A Batch

of

Patchwork

Beyond the Quilting Bee

12 Easy Quilts to Make with Friends

by May T. Miller

and

Susan B. Burton

Located in Paducah, Kentucky, the American Quilter's Society (AQS), is dedicated to promoting the accomplishments of today's quilters. Through its publications and events, AQS strives to honor today's quiltmakers and their work — and inspire future creativity and innovation in quiltmaking.

EDITOR: CYNDY RYMER
TECHNICAL EDITOR: BONNIE K. BROWNING
BOOK DESIGN/ILLUSTRATIONS: LANETTE BALLARD
COVER DESIGN: TERRY WILLIAMS
PHOTOGRAPHY: CHARLES R. LYNCH

Library of Congress Cataloging-in-Publication Data
Miller, May T.
        A batch of patchwork : beyond the quilting bee, 12 easy quilts to
    make with friends … / by May T.Miller and Susan B. Burton.
                        p.   cm.
        ISBN 0-89145-883-2
        1. Patchwork--Patterns.   2. Quilting--Patterns.   I. Burton, Susan
T.   II. Title.
TT835.B885   1997
746.46'041--dc21   97-36647
                                                        CIP

Additional copies of this book may be ordered from: American Quilter's Society, PO Box 3290, Paducah, KY 42002-3290 @ $18.95. Add $2.00 for postage & handling.

Printed in the U.S.A. by Image Graphics, Paducah, KY

Contents

Dedication

To my late mother who taught by example there is nothing you can't do.

And to my husband, Bob, who gave his full support and never stood in my way.

May T. Miller

For my mother, Barbara B. Butts, who has marked each milestone in my life with a quilt.

Susan B. Burton

Acknowledgments

Starting my shop in a vacant feed store
I thought I'd be cold forever more.

But thanks to good folks in our small town
I've managed so far to stick around.

My husband came through with 30 cords for the fire
So I could stitch quilts to my heart's desire.

Work with me all day? They said no one could do it.
Happily Betty and Babs have stuck right to it.

Thanks to my students as I bluffed my way through
Little did I know how much I'd learn from you.

From the feed store to my chicken house on the hill,
Mike got me here with his carpenter's skills.

Susan and her computer have redone and corrected,
But somehow or other we've stayed connected.

May T. Miller

To so many great people I owe words of praise
As they've helped us through to publishing day.

'Twas May's great idea for a book, what fun!
Little did we know – so much work to be done.

Ken's patient forbearance through night and day
As I spent many hours typing away.

When Sarah was playing I'd hear her say – "Look!
Elmo, be quiet, Mommy's writing her book."

My mom kept me going and kept stitching away,
My dad gladly took Sarah and played many a day.

To family and friends who babysat, sewed, or cooked,
We give this to you, our first quilting book.

Susan B. Burton

Introduction

"Oh! I'd love to have a quilt but I don't have the time or the patience." "No! Not me! I can't sew." "Are you kidding? I'd never finish. I've started many classes and never finished anything." "I'd love to give her a quilt for a wedding gift, but I'd never get one done."

Having owned a quilt shop for years, I've heard all the reasons why people just can't make a quilt. Yet it seemed to me that by using the rotary cutter and innovative shortcuts that have become commonplace in the world of quilting, there had to be a way to help folks stitch the quilts they longed to make.

Since the days of the American pioneers, quilters have worked together. Quilting bees brought women together to share the burden of quilting their pieced quilts, making what was a task a pleasure. Why not gather to piece quilt tops, too?

With this in mind, the principle of assembly lines, a few quilting shortcut techniques, and the get-to-work ethic fostered during years of dairy farming were combined. What developed were easy-to-follow instructions for traditional quilt patterns made so handily that three people, spending just three days, can produce three quilt tops ready to tie or quilt. In my shop, I added quick lunches and snacks to keep energy levels up and the class was a hit!

The quilt directions in this book are tried and true. The instructions are written for three people, but you can also tackle any of the quilts on your own. The shortcuts and quick cutting instructions will make your quilt go together beautifully.

In addition to instructions for 12 quilts, this book contains tips and instructions on choosing fabrics, cutting, stitching, pressing, borders, backing, binding, tying, and quilting. Take a few minutes to read over the tips before you start each step to save a lot of time. Be sure and check out the last chapter for some of our favorite recipes.

Have fun, forget the calories, and enjoy each other's company!

Chapter 1

Patterns, Tools, Fabrics, and Workspace

Getting Started

Quilt pattern
Look through the 12 quilts included in this book and choose one you like. Read through the directions carefully to get a feel for what you will be doing and take the book with you when you go to buy your fabric.

Fabric
Read the section in this chapter on choosing colors and material; check the yardage needed for your chosen pattern. Then head to a fabric store.

Tools
Though you may be overwhelmed by the number of tools available to quilters of the '90s, you will need only a few to start. As you become more familiar with quiltmaking, you'll decide what works best for you. You will need sharp scissors, pins, and several spools of a good quality thread, either cotton or cotton covered polyester in a complementary color.

Since you will be working with different color fabrics, to avoid switching thread, a pewter color almost always works. Other tools needed include a rotary cutter with a sharp blade and a safety cover, a cutting board for the rotary cutter, and at least one clear plastic quilting ruler (preferably 6" x 24") with 60° and 45° angles, and ⅛", ¼", ½", and 1" lines clearly marked. You may also want to invest in a large square (12" – 16") ruler.

If you are tying your quilt, you will need crochet cotton and large-eyed needles. If you're planning on hand quilting, purchase special quilting thread, quilting needles, a thimble, and a marking tool that will show on your quilt. A thin lead mechanical pencil is used whenever possible.

Space
Whether working alone or with a group, you'll need space to call your own, a pressing table or ironing board, a sewing machine, and a cutting table. Access to a quilting frame or a large open area on a rug-covered floor will also be needed.

Adequate light in all your workspace will make work easier. Have a variety of chairs available to give the opportunity to switch chairs if your back or arms begin to ache.

Working in a group
If you are working in a group, be sure at least one person can use a sewing machine. Have each person select a quilt pattern; each person furnishes fabric for his or her quilt. Schedule four sessions that everyone can attend. (We usually schedule sessions a week apart to allow time to recuperate and dissipate the calories from the previous session!)

The goal is to complete a quilt top each day for the first three sessions; on the fourth day, the group will tie or baste each quilt. The only things that are done away from class are choosing and preparing the fabric, preparing the back, and quilting and binding the quilt. (And wouldn't it be fun to get together again for the quilting?)

If this project is taught as a class, limit the groups to what you have room for in your shop or home. If several groups are working at the same time, it is best if each group is making the same quilt on any given day.

Set out coffee, tea, and cookies. Sooner or later everyone finds a minute to help themselves without holding up the production line. Each person in the group of three has a specific role to play. The stitcher is "queen of the day." The other two will not only keep work laid out in front of her, ready to be stitched, but also will bring refreshments to keep up her spirits.

You can do these quilts alone, though you may not get a top done in just one day. Anyway, piecing a quilt is more fun when the task is shared. Why not grab a couple of friends or relatives, set up a few days without children, spouses, and other responsibilities, and working together, each of you will end up with a lovely quilt top in just three days.

Sustenance
If you are planning to work all day on your quilt as we suggest, be sure to plan easy, non-messy snacks, and lunch. A suggested lunch menu is included with each chapter to give you an idea of foods to include in your classes. Recipes for these and some snacks are in the last chapter of this book.

Positive attitude
You can make a quilt! There is power in positive thinking, so approach each project knowing that if you follow these directions, you will finish your quilt. Your potential for success increases dramatically if you join forces with friends who are also excited about their quilts. Many people in our classes who have never completed a quilt before or done much sewing of any kind have been delighted with their quilts!

Choosing and Preparing Your Fabrics

Choosing the fabric for your quilt can seem like an overwhelming task, but it can be lots of fun if you do not allow yourself to be overwhelmed. By following a few steps, you can end up with a quilt you love. The basics — consider where the quilt will be used, choose colors you like, and take your time!

Your fabric personalizes your quilt. You've seen quilts you like better than others, so what makes the difference between a Log Cabin that you are dying to take home and one that really does not appeal? Usually it's the fabric choice — the same pattern can have a very different look depending on the fabrics.

> **Helpful Tip**
> Are you planning to hand quilt your masterpiece? Stick to plainer fabrics in the big spaces on your quilt so you will have a perfect place to stitch a lovely design. Or choose a fabric with a design in these big spaces that you can easily quilt around. If you are hand quilting, one big border is sufficient and sensible because it leaves space for a more elaborate hand-quilted design.

Where the quilt will be used
Before buying your fabric, take a good look at what will surround the quilt. If you are making a quilt for your guest room decorated in burgundy, cream, and navy blue, you probably don't want to make an orange and green quilt. But if you are making it for your teenage son or grandson who has a black light and camouflage walls, he might just love the orange and green — be sure to throw in a little purple just for fun!

You are the color expert
Follow your tastes, not someone else's. You may want advice from friends or the quilters running the fabric store, and they may be able to help you. But remember that you have to like the quilt. Others may choose colors that are lovely, but if you do not like them, your quilt will not be right.

There is not a right or wrong way to choose quilt colors. The color wheel is a useful tool for choosing complementary colors and finding nice combinations, but it should not rule you. Making quilts is an art and art is subjective. Dare to be different and follow your own aesthetic sense.

If you are unsure of what you want, look around for some guidance. There may be a lovely print dress that you adore or a piece of upholstery material that is a perfect mix of colors. Maybe your best friend just hung the most beautiful drapes in her living room and you want those colors in your quilt. Take an ample piece of the fabric to the quilt shop and use it to guide you when choosing colors. (Your friend will never notice the hole in her drapes if you make it in a fold!) If you use the colors in something you've seen, chances are you will like the quilt and it will really be you!

Do not rush

Take your time when choosing fabric. It is hard to pop into the store on your lunch hour, pull out the perfect six fabrics from the huge number available, figure how much you need, buy it, and get back to work before the boss notices you are gone. Plan to spend an afternoon browsing through the fabrics, trying different combinations of colors, and finding the special something that will make your quilt unique.

Fabric content

Most fabric sold as quilting material is 100% cotton and that is what is recommended. Polyester/cotton blends are available and some may prefer them since they may fade or wrinkle less. However, poly/cotton may pill with use and the edges may ravel more than cotton. Do not mix cotton and polyester/cotton fabrics in the same quilt.

Everyone loves a bargain; however, don't substitute a bargain for quality. Too much work is put into a quilt. Keep in mind it is a future heirloom, so don't skimp on fabric.

> **Helpful Tips**
> If you do use poly/cottons in your quilt, allow for a bigger seam. Instead of the ¼" seam in these directions, use ⅜" to make up for raveling that will occur. Be sure to buy a little extra fabric to allow for this seam increase.

For purely decorative quilts or wall hangings that will not be machine laundered, anything goes — silks, rayons, voiles. Only your imagination limits you. For purely functional quilts our ancestors used whatever they had available: wools, old clothes, anything they could get their hands on, as long as the fabric was durable.

Are you in the mood?

The mood you want to create has a great deal to do with your color scheme. You may want a flowery, Victorian feeling, something light and airy, or something strong and masculine. To achieve a warm look, use dark, rich roses, reds, or yellows. For a cool look, go with breezy blues, whites, and other light colors. You may be a person who likes the homespun, country look or someone who craves elegance. Stick to one mood in your quilt. Mixing moods may not give you the effect you like; it can be difficult to make muslin and an exotic metallic fabric look right together.

It doesn't have to match exactly

People sometimes try to match all their fabric colors exactly. For instance, they want a fabric to be the exact shade of a color in their drapes or wallpaper. Chances are, if you match all the colors in your fabrics too closely, your quilt will be lifeless and dull.

Use different intensities, try a big print, use a shaded fabric, throw in a black, brown, or gray to add life. Yes, gray can add life to your quilt — a neutral color may lift your ordinary quilt to the realms of the extraordinary. It may provide a perfect backdrop for your stronger colors, and if placed appropriately in a quilt, it can be used to emphasize the pattern you wish to bring to the forefront.

Placement is important

Once you have chosen the fabrics, decide on color placement in your quilt. Color placement emphasizes different patterns. Bright and light colors will make the pattern come forward, whereas a darker color will recede and recess the pattern.

The following three pictures show the Rings of Color quilt in three different fabric combinations. Notice how the different fabrics change the look and mood of the quilt.

8

Rings of Color #1

In this quilt a lovely large floral print ties the rings together. The shades of teal and rose complement the floral and the three narrow borders (which make up the first 6¾" border called for in the instructions) frame the rings nicely. In this instance, the same fabric was used for Colors #2 and #4. The overall effect is flowery and light like a Victorian garden path.

Rings of Color #2

This is a dark, rich quilt that creates an aura of sultry mystery. The sharp contrast between colors brings the pink rings to the forefront. Notice how different this is from the first quilt as the rings in that quilt capture your attention equally. In this example, the dark blues and greens surround the pink and put them on center stage.

Rings of Color #3

The colors in this quilt suggest the change of season as fall gives way to winter. The wildlife motif fits this mood and may make it a perfect quilt for the man or boy in your life.

Using several smaller borders helps tie all the colors together, and framing it in the dark blue fabric helps prevent the border from discoloring with use.

Rather than use the deer print in the small blocks in the Nine-Patch miniature block, the fabric used was the same color as the deer print background. To do this, ¾ yard was used for the small squares and 1½ yards for the large squares.

A Batch of Patchwork

Here are some samples of partial layouts of the Split Rail or Knot pattern that also show how color and fabric placement can change your quilt.

Split Rail #1 – This is the basic Split Rail layout where fabrics go from dark to light and light to dark in the final blocks.

Split Rail #2 – The Split Rail layout is the same but the blocks are different. When sewing the strips that make these blocks, a strong color is placed on each side of the strip set. Thus, the blocks do not go from light to dark/dark to light. The look of the overall quilt is very different.

Split Rail #3 – In this sample, the fabrics are placed light to dark and dark to light within the blocks. However, a blue fabric, is added in place of the red used in the other layouts. This provides a more gentle blending of colors that may be more pleasing to the eye.

Photographer, pages 10-18: Sally Alvarez

A Batch of Patchwork

Knot #1 – These blocks are the same as in the Split Rail #1 layout with the fabric placed from dark to light and light to dark.

Knot #3 – In this final sample, the fabrics are placed light to dark and dark to light within the blocks, using the blue fabric instead of the red. (These are the same blocks used in Split Rail #3.)

Knot #2 – The fabrics in these squares are the same as in Knot #1 but reorganized so there is a strong color on each side of the block. There is no light to dark/dark to light sequence. (These are the same blocks as in the Split Rail #2 layout.)

Shaded fabrics and stripes can add pizazz to a quilt.

Choosing your border fabric

Borders give your quilt a finished look and frame your masterpiece. The border color is usually chosen from those used in your quilt or from ones that complement. Quite often the best fabrics to use in the border are your favorites throughout the quilt. Repeating a fabric in the border makes it a stronger contributor to the entire picture you are creating.

Sometimes it helps the whole quilt to use a fabric for the border that has been used only sparingly throughout the quilt. It makes that fabric look like it really belongs. If you find a stripe or other fabric you love which does not lend itself to piecing, you might choose that just for the border and coordinate your quilt colors with it.

Remember to consider whether your quilt will be tied or hand quilted when planning your borders. If you are hand quilting a big elaborate design, a wide, plain border will look best.

If you like the look of several borders but don't want to piece them, choose a wide stripe for your border for a similar effect — it's a lot quicker! See page 80 for a Double Irish Chain quilt which uses a striped border.

Putting a darker border on the outside creates a frame around the quilt that can look good. It also helps protect the edges of the quilt from discoloration from use.

> **Helpful Tip**
> To add flair and color to your quilt, try using one of the shaded fabrics available. In one yard of fabric there can be many different colors! Stripes can also be fun. If your fabric has two or more different designs in the stripes, you can use each one as a separate entity, adding variety to your pattern.

The border also plays an important role in determining the size of your quilt. Instructions for the quilts in this book tell you how big the quilt is before the border and then suggests border sizes for double and queen size quilts. You can add extra or larger borders, or subtract borders from your quilt to get it just the size you want.

Choosing your binding fabric

Usually the quilt is bound with the same fabric used in the outside border as a continuation of the border. However, you may want to re-emphasize a different color with the binding, creating a final, smaller border. Instructions with the quilt patterns recommend buying enough fabric to make the binding double thickness which helps your quilt wear better.

Choosing your backing fabric

If you are planning to hand quilt, choose a plain back, one that will provide a canvas for your decorative quilting. If you are planning to tie your quilt, the choice is yours, as long as your backing choice complements the front of your quilt. Choose something you love that will look pretty, elegant, or festive on those days when you don't make your bed and the back is there for all the world to see.

The instructions give yardage requirements for backing in 44/45" fabric widths. You will need to seam this fabric to back your quilt. There are also many pretty fabrics in 90" or 108" widths that are perfect for quilt backs. If you find this wider backing material, purchase yardage the length of your quilt, adding a couple extra inches to both the width and

length measurements to be sure your quilt back is larger than your top.

Note: If you are going to lap the back over the front instead of adding a binding, allow 6 extra inches on each side.

How much fabric to buy?

Each quilt in this book is designed in both double and queen sizes and all the measurements are listed at the beginning of the pattern explanation. Take this book along and you should not have any trouble buying what you need. Remember that the yardage is figured for 44/45" width fabric so you will have to do some figuring if your material is a different width. Beware! Some fabrics are actually a couple inches shy of 44". You will need to buy extra yardage if you choose a narrower fabric.

All beds are different, so be sure to measure your specific bed before you decide what size your quilt should be. Take a tape measure and measure across the mattress, allowing for the amount you want to hang over each side. The thickness of your mattress and box springs, and height of the bed itself all contribute to the variation between beds.

> **Helpful Tips**
> Most of these directions will work for twin-size quilts. Just note the "Size Before Border" in the individual directions and add only the border needed to fit your twin bed. You can also use some of these instructions for crib-size quilts; you'll just need to reduce the size of your pieces. For example, to do the Trip Around the World in a crib size, note that the size before the border is 60½" x 82½". If you cut those dimensions in half and add a 3" border, you'll have a quilt just right for a baby. So, instead of using 6" blocks, use 3" blocks!
>
> All of these quilts are sewn with ¼" seam allowances throughout. Be sure you sew a consistent ¼". See page 16 for further instructions.

Many people with a king size bed find that a queen size quilt is ample. Remember the corners will hang lower than the sides, and the length can vary depending on if you want to tuck the quilt under the pillows or if you have oversized pillows. Adjustments can be made by changing your border widths or leaving some of the border off the top of the quilt that will be tucked behind the pillows.

Preparing your fabric

Most quilt directions and books suggest washing fabrics before sewing. Unless a fabric will run when washed, some prefer to work with fabric that has not been washed.

Follow these simple steps to determine if your fabric runs. Before starting your quilt, take a small sample of each fabric and sew each on a piece of white fabric of the same fiber content. Put each sample in a clear glass of warm water; the water should just cover the top of the fabric. Leave it a minute, then swirl it around. If even one fabric colors the water, wash all your fabrics. You don't want to wash just one of your fabrics as it may shrink differently than the unwashed. You don't want to put time and effort into a quilt that will pucker and pull in the first wash! When washing a piece that runs, continue to dip it in clean water until the water stays clear. For a stubborn piece, try soaking it in a solution of 5 pints water and 1 pint vinegar.

Helpful Tips

Another way to determine if a fabric is colorfast is to wet a small piece of it and stitch it to a piece of white cloth. If the colors have bled after it is dry, you will want to prewash all your fabric.

———————

Save scraps of white fabric so you'll always have a bit of white to put in the water with the dark fabric scraps when checking for color fastness.

———————

Don't buy your batting until you're sure what size your quilt will be! If you plan to use your quilt on a queen size bed, but want it extra long or wide, you may need to buy king size batting and cut it down.

Batting sizes: Twin – 72" x 90"
Double – 91" x 96"
Queen – 90" x 108"
King – 120" x 120"

Chapter 2

Basics of Cutting, Sewing, and Pressing

Cutting

The quilts in this book are made using the rotary cutter and plastic rulers so popular among quilters now. If you do not have either tool of your own, browse through quilt shops and talk to quilters. Find out which tools they like best and why. Every quilter prefers certain types and you will discover yours as you go along. We recommend you have a sharp rotary cutter, a cutting mat, a clear ruler, a clear square ruler, and a pair of sewing scissors.

In most of these quilts, the strips are cut across the width of the fabric. It will be stated clearly if that is not the case. When starting to cut your fabric, it is important to lay it out carefully and be sure it is smooth before cutting. Lay it out and then fold it over so you will not have to make a long cut. It is easier to hold the more narrow pieces tightly with your ruler.

Before you cut strips or squares, be sure that you even up any rough ends or cut off the selvage if you are working from a finished edge. To do this trimming, place the ruler on the fabric leaving the selvage or rough edges showing. Line up the markers on your ruler with the fold of the fabric. Hold ruler steady with your left hand (if you are right handed) and cut with your right. If you happen to be left-handed, reverse the process. Position the ruler so that you cut off just enough — the entire selvage or all the uneven edges — without wasting fabric, so your edge is straight. You will need to turn the fabric around to cut the fabric into strips.

The cut is a firm steady stroke — push the cutter away from you and make the cut in one motion. Hold the cutter firmly and straight up and down; you do not want a wobbly edge (Step 1). If you have never used a rotary cutter before, practice several cuts on a scrap of material.

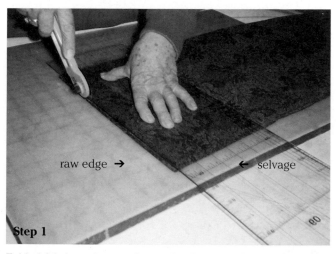

raw edge →   ← selvage

Step 1

Folded fabric makes cutting easier. In most of the quilts in this book, you will fold your fabric to cut off the raw edges first as shown here.

To cut strips after cutting off the edges, move your ruler so the amount of fabric you need to cut is firmly underneath the ruler with your fabric extending to the right. Then cut with your right hand along the edge in a firm, steady motion (Step 2). If you don't cut through completely the first time, you can go back and carefully recut the entire length, but be certain to hold the ruler steady.

When you have multiple strips sewn together that need to be cut into strips across the seams, be certain to line up the marks on your ruler with the seams, not with the edges. Cut off uneven edges or selvages (Step 3).

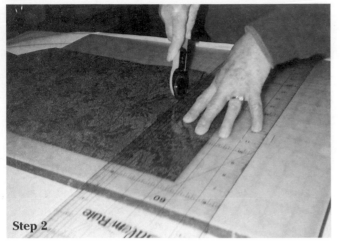
Step 2

Holding the ruler firmly with the width of the strip you are cutting underneath the ruler, cut fabric with your rotary cutter.

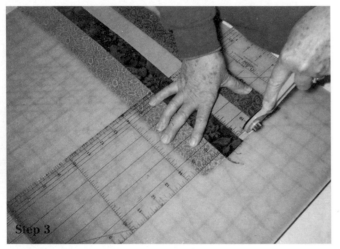
Step 3

Cut off uneven selvages before you cut your strips into pieces. Be sure to line up the ruler with the seams you have sewn, not the edges of the fabric. This photo shows the hand positions if you are left handed.

Helpful Tips

If you are working with a long piece of cloth, either fold it to make your cut shorter or use a ruler that is longer than the fabric you're cutting. You can move the ruler as you make the cut but it is easier to make a clean cut without moving it. It's easier to move your hand along the longer ruler.

Safety first! Always put the guard back on your rotary cutter after making the cut.

Line up the ruler marks with the seams and cut as indicated in the instructions for your particular quilt (Step 4). After you have cut a few pieces, realign the ruler to make sure you are not going askew.

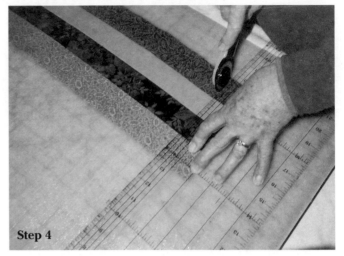
Step 4

When cutting your fabric into smaller pieces, be sure to realign the ruler to the seam line every few cuts.

Helpful Tip

When quilt making —
There's no such thing as always.
There's no such thing as never.
Now always remember that
And never forget it.

Sewing

The key to good quilt sewing is a straight, true seam. All the instructions in this book use a ¼" seam. To see if your seam is a true ¼", test yourself with the following:

- Fold a piece of ¼" grid paper on a line.
- Lower the needle onto a line.
- Without watching the line on the paper, sew what you think is a ¼" seam, right through the paper.
- If your seam stays right on the line, then you're right on.
- If the stitches hit on one side or the other, you'll need to adjust your seam size.

It may help to mark the ¼" mark on your machine with a strip of masking tape to keep your seams consistent.

Another important factor to your sewing success is your comfort. Be sure your chair is the right height so you are not leaning over too far, making your back ache, or reaching up with your hands, tiring your arms unnecessarily. If you get tired, switch chairs, get up, stretch legs, back, and arms, and move around for a minute.

Adjust your stitch length to a smaller than average stitch to make your quilt seams more secure. Remember, too, you don't usually take time to backstitch when piecing a quilt. Simply run your seams off the edge of your fabric. In many of the instructions you simply feed pairs of pieces through one after the other without lifting the presser foot. This is a great time saver and can be used in many projects to speed up your work.

> **Helpful Tip**
> Want to sew a perfect ¼" seam? Use a piece of grid paper as your guide! Fold the paper, put your needle down on a line. As you sew down the paper, see where the next line lies in relation to your presser foot.

Backstitch your final edge seams (the ones that will meet the borders). This will make them stronger and less likely to pull apart when stretching your quilt to meet the border. You will also need to backstitch when putting on your borders and binding as noted in the instructions for those steps.

Pressing

Good pressing is essential to a quality product. You'll need a good, clean iron adjusted for cotton fabrics and a firm, clean pressing table or ironing board. Be sure your table or board is padded for

extra smoothness. If you have room, pad a piece of 4' x 8' plywood (or as big a piece as you have room for) with cotton batting and cover the whole thing tightly with a sheet or muslin. Set this up on sawhorses for a very effective ironing table.

When pressing, especially blocks with bias edges, pick the iron up and set it down firmly on your piece rather than sliding the iron. This helps keep the fabric from stretching, makes your quilt pieces more accurate, and assures you are happy with the finished product. For added accuracy in pressing individual pieces, press the stitched seam flat before opening to press in any direction.

In some of the instructions, you will press the seams in a specific direction. Often you will press the seams toward the darkest fabric so the seam does not show. Or you may alternate the direction you are pressing by row so your seams do not end up on top of each other, leaving a bulky seam that is difficult to quilt. Use common sense, considering what colors you are using, and whether you are going to be quilting the finished product. For instance, if you are quilting a Log Cabin and you want to quilt "in the ditch," along the inside of each seam instead of through the bulky seams, you may not want to alternate the directions of your seams. Alternate pressing of the seams would make you jump from one ditch to the next rather than giving you a nice straight quilting line.

> **Helpful Tip**
> To keep strip sets straighter when pressing, draw a straight line on your ironing board with a permanent marking pen. Line your sets up with the line to make pressing straight a snap!

Strip set pressing

One of the most important times good pressing is

necessary is when you have sewn your sets of strips together. The following few steps will help.

Step 1

The first step is to take each strip set, and without opening it completely, lay it on your pressing table. Press each seam flat as it was sewn (Step 1).

Step 2

Open the strip set and press the seams lightly toward the dark fabric (usually) on the *wrong* side of the fabric (Step 2).

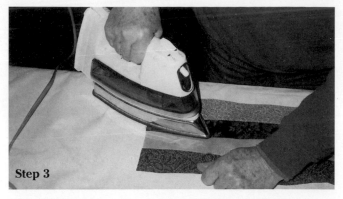

Step 3

Turn the strip over and with right side up, press the strip set to its fullest possible width (Step 3). When pressing the strip set, use the edge of the table as your guide, keeping the edge of the strip set the same distance from the edges of the table for the entire length of the set. Or draw a straight line on your ironing board to use as a guide to help press a straight set.

Following the illustrations

Throughout this book, color illustrations are used to serve as a visual guide as you construct your quilt. The right side of the fabrics is shown in color, while the wrong side of the fabrics is shown in gray scale. So, if you see the gray coloring, you will know that the piece or unit should be wrong side up.

Chapter 3

Borders, Backing, and Batting

Borders

The most important things to remember when cutting and applying the border is that you must measure the quilt before cutting the border and that you want to keep your quilt square. With this in mind, follow these steps to determine what length to cut your borders:

- Start with the sides of your quilt. Holding the quilt taut, measure two of the seams (not the edge of your quilt top) and take the average of those two measurements (Fig. 1).

Fig. 1

Measure the length of two of these seams, not the edge of the quilt. Take the average and cut two borders to that length for the sides of your quilt. These can be cut from the length or the width of your fabric, but the fabric stretches less when cut with the length (selvage).

- Cut two border strips this length in the desired width.
- Pin the strips to the sides of the quilt with the border on top, right sides together. Holding them firmly, pin the edges of border and quilt together, keeping the edges even, then stretch to fit, and pin in the middle. Stretch to fit between two of the pins and pin in the middle of the two pins, continuing until there is a pin about every six inches. (In order to stretch and pin, you may need to hold an edge of the quilt with your teeth or your toes or your elbows. It helps to do the pinning with a friend).
- Carefully machine sew the borders onto the sides of your quilt top, backstitching at the beginning and the end of your seam for added strength.
- When the two side borders have been applied, press the seam toward the borders. Again holding the quilt taut, measure the width of the quilt and these two side borders at two of the seams and take the average of these measurements (Fig. 2).

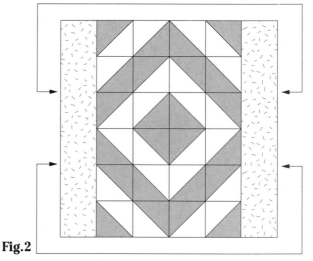

Fig. 2

Measure the length of two of these seams across the width of the quilt, plus the borders you have added. Take the average and cut two borders to that length for the top and bottom of your quilt.

Helpful Tip

Be sure to have your quilt top completed before you cut the border fabric. No one sews the same ¼" seam and your quilt may have turned out to be a slightly different size than the instructions.

- Cut two border strips this length in the desired width.
- Pin the strips at each end to the top and bottom of the quilt as you did for the side borders, and, holding them carefully, stretch to fit, and pin in the middle. Stretch to fit between two of the pins and pin in the middle, continuing until there is a pin about every six inches.
- Carefully machine sew the borders onto the top and bottom of your quilt top, backstitching at the beginning and the end of your seam for added strength.
- Repeat the process to apply additional borders.

If you find your fabric yardage works out better putting your end borders on first, go for it!

Sizing with borders

Borders can be used to make your quilt just the right size. You can add extra borders or make larger borders if you want to make your quilt bigger. You can add an extra border on an end to make it longer or leave off the upper border, which will be tucked behind the pillows, if you need a shorter quilt. If possible, measure the actual bed for which the quilt is being made. Though the length and width measurements of modern mattresses are standard, beds vary in size depending on the thickness of the mattress, box springs, and the height of the frame. Using a tape measure, figure the length you want your quilt to hang over the edges, keeping in mind that the quilt will hang longer at the corners. Then determine the width border you need for the perfect size, and whether you want one or multiple borders.

Backing

The backing yardage given with all patterns in this book is figured using 44/45" fabric. However, there

This border style is more effective.

This border is not as easy on the eye.

Helpful Tip

If you like multiple borders, decide what size borders you need to make the quilt size you want, cut the sections, and sew them together. You will have several borders in one strip, and you can apply them all at once. Other options could be to miter your corners or add a square in the corners.

Helpful Tip

When making your quilt back, be sure you make it several inches larger than your quilt on all sides! This makes finishing easier and safer since the layers may shift a bit when being sandwiched.

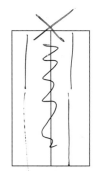 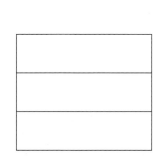

Double Quilt Back
Two lengths
of 44/45" fabric,
seamed vertically.

Queen Quilt Back
Three strips
of 44/45" fabric joined
with two horizontal seams.

Fig. 3

are some really nice 60", 90", and 108" fabrics available that may be perfect for your quilt back. These widths make preparing your backing easy for you — often requiring only one seam or even no seams across the back.

Measure your quilt, and add about 4" to all sides. (If you plan to bring the back of the quilt around to the front instead of adding a binding, add 6" to all sides.) Figure how much fabric will be needed. For a double quilt, you usually can simply sew two strips of material together so the seam is vertical down the back of the quilt. With a queen size quilt, you will probably want to put three strips of fabric across the back, making two horizontal seams. If you are running short on fabric, the back can be pieced to fit. An extra seam or two will not hurt.

Batting

Batting is available in different thicknesses or lofts as it is called in the quilting world. The higher the loft, the warmer and puffier your quilt will be. If you are planning to quilt your quilt, either by hand or machine, you will want a light- to medium-weight loft. It is difficult to put a small hand stitch in a thick batting. If you are tying your quilt, you can use any loft — low is for summer weight, medium will be slightly heavier and warmer, and the highest loft will give you more of a comforter-type quilt.

Batting is also made from a variety of fibers and fiber combinations. Polyester batting is readily available in quilting and craft shops and it works well for tied quilts because of the fluffy loft. Some people prefer cotton batting but it is harder to quilt through than the polyester batting. However, try a sample piece of your choice. Manufacturers are working with cotton to make it easier to hand quilt. Some other types available are wool and milkweed silk.

Chapter 4

Finishing Your Quilt

To Tie or Quilt, That is the Question

Almost everyone can appreciate the beauty of a quilted quilt, especially a hand-quilted masterpiece. If you love quilting, you may want to quilt several quilts in your life. However, in this day and age, many of us do not have time to hand quilt. Long winter evenings and dreary rainy afternoons are good times to work on quilting. Quilt tops can be pieced faster than they can be quilted, so some quilts can be tied, too. Do what you like and have time to do. You may want to quilt an exceptionally beautiful quilt and tie the quick quilt you put together to go on your child's bed. You may do your own machine quilting if that is your thing or you can find someone with a large industrial quilting machine to do it for you (ask your local quilt shop for recommendations). Regardless of what you decide, there is a place in our hearts for each and every quilt.

The Quilting Frame

Whether you are going to quilt or tie, it really helps to have a quilting frame available. If you don't have a frame of your own, many quilt shops will let you use their frames to baste your layers together or tie your quilt. If frames are available, follow any directions for that specific frame. The old-fashioned frames are basic and usually consist of four wooden bars, covered with fabric for easy pinning, held together with C-clamps. This basic quilting frame will be used for the purpose of discussion.

Measure your quilt top and clamp the bars together so the frame is the same size as your quilt top. Pin the backing of your quilt, wrong side up, onto the frame, hanging equal amounts of material over each side of the frame. Pin it on tautly and do not skimp on pins. Put the pins in from the outside, points toward the center of the quilt.

Lay the batting on top of the back, making sure it falls beyond the edge of the frame. You don't have to pin this layer. Then lay the quilt top on, right side up. Using plenty of pins, pin the top on tightly. Stick your pins all the way through to the bars to keep all your layers secure (Fig. 4).

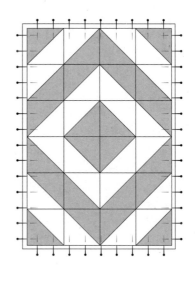

Fig. 4

What to do if you don't have a quilting frame at your fingertips

Assembling a quilt can be done without a quilting frame but it is a little more difficult. You will need a clear space on a carpeted floor with enough room for your quilt to lie flat and allow plenty of room to work around all sides. Or, you can use a large table (ping-pong sized works well) which is easier to work on because you do not have to crawl around on the floor, but it doesn't allow you to work as tightly when putting your quilt together.

If you are working on the floor, stretch the quilt backing out right side down and pin it to the rug. Make it taut by sticking pins at angles into the carpet. Leave space between the pins to allow you to insert an 8" x 11" piece of cardboard under the quilt to use when basting or tying your quilt. Lay the batting on top of the backing, then the quilt top, right side up. Pin the entire unit to the rug.

Once pinned, you can baste or tie as instructed in the following sections. Place the piece of cardboard under the quilt as you work your needle so the rug does not interfere with your progress. You will not be able to reach the center of your quilt from the edge so just climb right on top (be sure to take your shoes off first). Baste or tie from the center out.

Tying

Before tying, take a look at your spread-out quilt and decide where you will make your ties. A good rule of thumb is to place your ties no more than 6" apart. You may wish to tie at the corners of some of your blocks, in the center, or in a pattern across the quilt — it's your call.

Start tying around the perimeter of the quilt, as far in as you can reach without hurting your back. Remember, it's better to roll the quilt a few more times than to stretch too far and hurt yourself. Be sure to stop and stretch as needed to keep yourself loose.

When you've tied as far as you can reach, remove the pins from the ends only as far as you have tied plus a pin or two. Make sure you leave the quilt pinned in the center for awhile.

If you're working on a quilting frame, two people are needed here, and each should grasp an end of a side bar. Keep the end of the bar against your body so you can pull on the side bar and keep the quilt taut. Carefully roll the quilt under, keeping it even, until the next work surface is readily accessible.

The ins and outs of tying

Crochet cotton of a medium weight (usually size 10) is recommended for tying. This is available in craft and quilting stores in many different colors. It might be available at a reasonable price in a discount department store as well. Some people use embroidery floss but it is a little slippery, may not hold the knots as well, and is usually more expensive. Common acrylic yarn is also a possibility but it may fuzz when washed, making your quilt look worn before its time.

Start with a long double thread of your crochet cotton, with no knot, on a needle. You will need a large needle with a good size eye to be able to thread the crochet cotton through it, but not so big that it is hard to push through the fabric. Send your needle down through the layers, take a ⅛" to ¼" stitch on the bottom and come straight back up. Use a thimble to make it easier to push the needle through the layers. Pull the thread so you have a couple of inches sticking up on the loose end for tying.

There are two ways to make your knots tight and secure. You can use a special square knot — cross your threads, right-over-left, wrap it around as in a normal square knot, but before you pull it tight, wrap it around again. Then tighten it down to the quilt top and follow through with a left-over-right cross and pull good and tight.

Clip your threads neatly at the desired length. What is the desired length? Whatever you want! You may not want them very long — several inches of thread ends may make your quilt look sloppy and increase the chance that the threads will get caught and your ties pulled loose.

However, a little thread is pretty and accents your quilt. About ¾" – 1¼" of thread ends is fine for most quilts.

The second way to put in a secure tie is to stitch twice in the same place. Thread your needle down through and back up as above, then go back down through in the same hole and come back up again before tying in a regular square knot.

Whichever method you choose, be consistent and tie your work tightly. The secret to longevity in a tied quilt is making secure knots.

Basting

If you're going to remove the quilt from your frame before you quilt it, you'll need to baste it carefully. If you're lucky enough to own a quilting frame, you can keep the quilt on it until it's all quilted; just pin the layers carefully every six inches or so around the perimeter as explained above and quilt it. No need to baste! To baste your quilt for lap quilting, just pin it to the frame as above. Then, with a long piece of thread on your needle, begin basting. (You may wish to use a curved needle for this.) Reach in as far as you can and baste out in straight lines, every four inches on all four sides of your quilt (the width of your hand is a good guide). At the corners, reach in from the point of the corner at a diagonal,

When you come to a corner, baste in diagonal lines as if you were dissecting pieces of pie. Continue to fill in holes until the stitch lines are 4" apart.

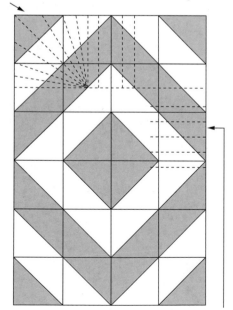

Reach in as far as you can, comfortably, and baste out. Baste about 4" apart along the edge of the quilt.

Fig. 5

pie fashion, and baste out toward the corner. Then continue stitching in diagonal lines until you've filled in the corner area (Fig. 5).

When you've basted as far as you can, remove the pins from the ends as far as you have basted plus a pin or two, leaving pins in the center. Again, two people are needed here; each should grasp an end of a side bar. Keep the end of the end bar against your body so you can pull on the side bar and keep the quilt taut. Carefully roll the quilt under, keeping it even, until your next work surface is readily accessible. Continue basting from the center out to your basted sections until the entire quilt is basted.

Quilting

Hand quilting can transform a quilt into a work of art and a precious heirloom. It takes many hours to do but can be therapeutic and marvelously satisfying as your hands stitch lovely designs in your patchwork.

The key to beautiful quilting is consistency. You may try to make tiny stitches but find that they are uneven, and the effect is not as lovely as you would like. Let yourself take a longer stitch but make it even, top and bottom, and you will be happier with the final product. Don't worry. The more you quilt the smaller your stitches will become.

Whether quilting on a frame or lap quilting, you will need a needle you are comfortable holding, quilting thread, and a thimble. Your needle can be short or long — buy a few to see which suits you best. Quilting needles are short and strong enough to withstand taking many stitches during the quilting process. One recommended style of thimble is one with a non-slip top to help hold your needle. There are many types of thimbles and finger covers available. Take a look at them; you may find one particularly appealing. However, you can certainly use any thimble that fits snugly, but not too tightly, and a few needles. Be sure to purchase thread designed especially for quilting.

Quilting thread is a little stronger and thicker than regular sewing thread and holds up well as you go in and out of the quilt layers.

Don't be tempted to thread a very long piece of thread for quilting; use no more than 18". Even quilting thread will wear out or tangle if pushed through the quilt too many times. Use a single thread and make a small knot. Come up through the back of the quilt where you want to start quilting. Gently work the knot through the back to lodge in the batting. Or skip the knot — start quilting in the opposite direction from the way you want to go; turn and go back exactly over those stitches and keep going.

When lap quilting, start in the center of your quilt and quilt out. You should go straight down into the quilt with your needle and then straight up a stitch length away, trying for even, not necessarily tiny, stitches. Your other hand is used to manipulate the quilt. Lap quilting is great to do on cold winter nights but can be a trial in the heat of the summer.

A running stitch is recommended — taking 3 – 6 stitches at a time on your needle, then pulling it through. A short needle is particularly helpful when quilting on a frame.

Use your other hand under the frame to help guide the needle and poke it back up. You are able to control your quilt more when lap quilting. It is harder to manipulate the needle when the quilt is pulled tight on the frame.

Binding

To prepare your quilt for binding after it is quilted or tied, trim the batting and backing to about an inch larger than your quilt tops.

- Measure around your quilt's perimeter, including the borders, to determine how many linear inches of binding you need to cut.
- Cut strips of the binding fabric as long as you can so you have fewer seams in the binding. Cut each strip at least 2¾" wide, and cut enough strips to go around the perimeter of your quilt plus 18".
- Sew your strips together end to end and press the seams, open this time.
- Fold in half lengthwise, keeping raw edges even and press evenly. This double layer of binding helps the edges of your quilt wear better.

Adding the Binding

Putting the binding on with these instructions should give you very neat, mitered corners.

Start sewing on the binding at a spot on the edge of

the quilt where the binding seams will not come too close to a corner. (You do not want any extra bulk in your corners.)

- Lay the raw edges of the binding along the raw edges of your quilt top.
- Starting about 4 or 5 inches from the end of the binding, stitch with a ⅜" seam to within ⅜" of the first corner (Fig. 6).
- Backstitch a few stitches.
- Remove the quilt from the machine and fold the ⅜" edge of the quilt which hasn't been sewn to the binding to the back.
- Take the free long end of the binding and fold it toward the back of the quilt, allowing the fold to extend about ½" beyond the last stitch.
- Keeping this fold straight and together, insert needle into the last stitch, being careful not to catch it in any of the quilt layers.
- Set your machine to a very short stitch length.
- Stitch an inverted V on the binding strip only as follows:
- Stitch diagonally toward the fold, ending the point of your V at the fold halfway between your seam and binding edge.
- Leaving your needle at the point of the V, turn your binding and stitch diagonally to the edge of the binding, ending exactly across from where you started your V. Backstitch (Fig. 7).
- Remove from the machine. Pivot your binding so the raw edge is again even with the raw edges of your quilt.
- Keeping the folded edge of the binding out of the way and the corner of the quilt flat, reinsert your needle at the end of the V and stitch a few stitches before returning your stitch length to the normal length (Fig. 8).
- Stitch to within ⅜" of the next edge and repeat this process at each corner of the quilt.
- As you come close to where you began, stop stitching and lay the 4 or 5 inches of binding you didn't sew straight along the edge of your quilt. Lay the other end of the binding on top, overlapping the first end by ¾" (Fig. 9).
- Cut any extra binding off, making sure you allow for a ¾" overlap.

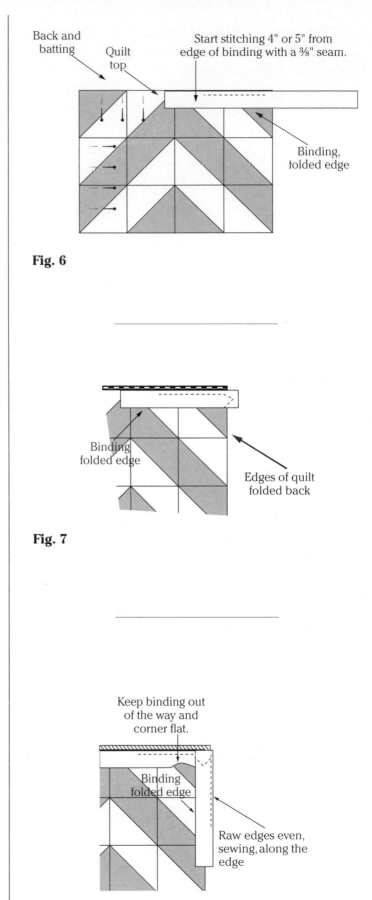

Fig. 6

Fig. 7

Fig. 8

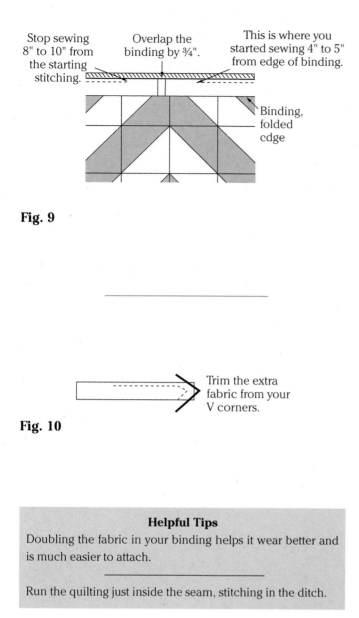

Stop sewing 8" to 10" from the starting stitching.

Overlap the binding by ¾".

This is where you started sewing 4" to 5" from edge of binding.

Binding, folded edge

Fig. 9

Trim the extra fabric from your V corners.

Fig. 10

Helpful Tips

Doubling the fabric in your binding helps it wear better and is much easier to attach.

Run the quilting just inside the seam, stitching in the ditch.

- Remove from the machine.
- Unfold the binding.
- With right sides together, sew the ends of the binding together using a ¾" seam. Finger press the seam open.
- Refold the binding and lay it on the quilt. Sew from the last stitching to the first.
- Trim excess batting and back even with the front. Trim extra fabric from your V corners (Fig. 10).
- Turn the binding corners right side out and stuff the quilt corners into them, carefully manipulating the corners so they are pointed and smooth.
- Hand stitch the folded edge of the binding to the back of the quilt.

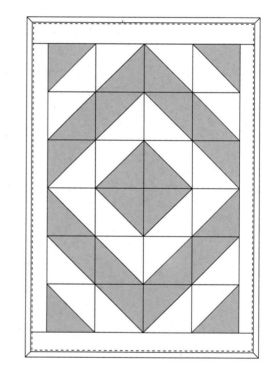

Some quilters prefer to make their quilt backing a little larger and bring it over to the front instead of adding a separate binding. If you do this, after you have hand stitched it to the front, add one line of hand quilting along the edge of the binding to ensure the batting is held securely to the edge.

Chapter 5

Projects

Pinwheel

Trip Around the World

Log Cabin

Split Rail or Knot

Amish Shadow

Pieces of Eight

English Log Cabin

Double Irish Chain

Rail Fence

Kissing Nine-Patch

Mock Jacob's Ladder

Rings of Color

Pinwheel Pattern

This quilt was inspired by Helen Whitsen Rose's "Windmill".

As seen in *Quilting with Strips and Strings*, Dover Needlework Series

Pinwheel

Quilt Sizes

Finished size double – 81" x 96", includes 6¾" border

Finished size queen – 90" x 105", includes 11¼" border

Size before border – 67½" x 82½"

Number of blocks – 71 (35 center, 36 outside)

Finished block size – 7½"

Finished border width double – one 6¾"

Finished border width queen – one 11¼" or one 7½" and one 3¾"

Fabric Selection

Color #3 is used for the connecting strip. You may want to try something bold and exciting here, such as one of the new large prints (those wonderful large florals or tropicals) you've been itching to try somewhere. You may also want to use the same fabric for the outside border to help tie your quilt together.

Block Samples

You'll end up with two different blocks. We'll call one a light block and one a dark.

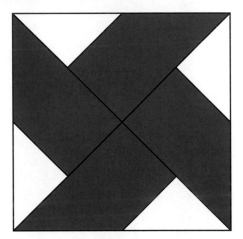

Dark Block

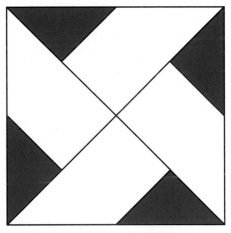

Light Block

Color Key

Color #1   Color #2   Color #3

Pinwheel

Layout Samples

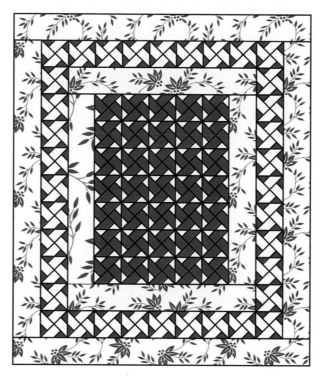

Made with Dark Blocks in center

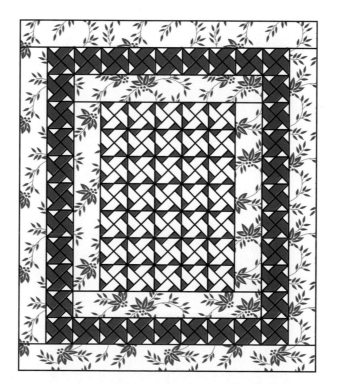

Made with Light Blocks in center

Pinwheel

Fabric Requirements (44/45" fabric)

Colors #1 and #2 – 2⅝ yards each

Color #3 – 1½ yards This is used for the connecting strip. If you are making a queen bed quilt with two borders, you might want to use the same fabric for the outside border.

	Double		Queen	
One Border	6¾"	2½ yards	11¼"	3½ yards
Two Borders	—	—	or { 3¾"	1½ yards &
			7½"	2½ yards
Binding	¾ yard		⅞ yard	
Backing	5¾ yards		8 yards	

Putting the team to work

Stitcher

Adjust your machine to a shorter than average stitch length because you will be cutting across seams. Try a seam on scrap fabric to get a ¼" seam and fill two or three bobbins with a neutral color thread.

Cutter

Fold your fabric and trim the raw edges (Chapter 2 for more details). Then cut one strip Color #1 and 1 strip Color #2, 3½" wide across the width of fabric.

Presser

Return these first two strips to the Stitcher.

Stitcher

With right sides together, sew these strips together along one long edge.

Presser

On the wrong side, press the seam flat, gently pressing the seam toward the darkest fabric. Flip to the right side, press to the fullest width, keeping the Strip Set as straight as possible.

Cutter

Cut 23 more 3½" strips of Color #1 and Color #2 as you did with the first two strips, alternating the colors.

Stitcher

Sew the remaining pairs of strips together.

Cutter

As strip sets are pressed, cut off the selvages. Measure across the width of the strip set and cut the strip into squares of this measurement, lining your ruler up with the seam line as in Fig. 11. You should be able to get six squares that are approximately 6½" from each strip set. You need a total of 144 squares. (After you have cut a few pieces, realign the ruler with the seam line in case you slip a bit.)

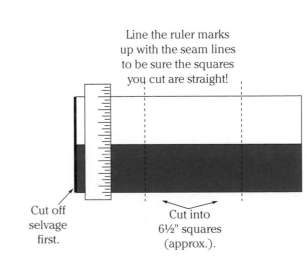

Line the ruler marks up with the seam lines to be sure the squares you cut are straight!

Cut off selvage first.

Cut into 6½" squares (approx.).

Fig. 11

32

A Batch of Patchwork

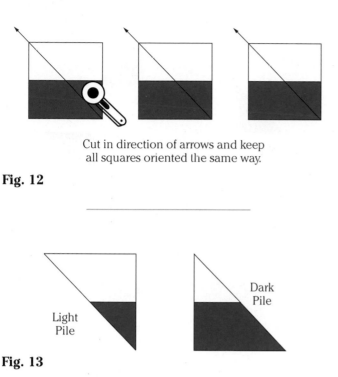

Cut in direction of arrows and keep all squares oriented the same way.

Fig. 12

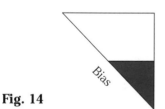

Light Pile

Dark Pile

Fig. 13

Bias

Bias

Fig. 14

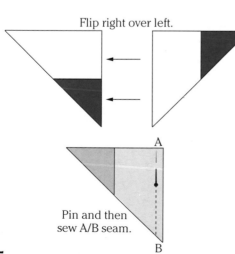

Flip right over left.

A

Pin and then sew A/B seam.

B

Fig. 15

Presser or Cutter

As time allows cut each square diagonally from the bottom right corner to the top left corner. Be sure always to have the same color toward you and always cut in the same direction. See Fig. 12.

Put these triangles into two piles — lights and darks — as in Fig. 13.

Cutter and Presser

Put aside the pile of dark triangles; start with the light pile. Using the light triangles, divide the pile in half as in Fig. 14.

* Return to this point for second set of blocks — see page 34.

Take the top triangle from each pile and flip the right one over onto the left. If stitcher has trouble keeping the blocks straight when sewing them, take an extra second or two to pin the seam that is to be sewn, with the point of the pin pointing to the place where she should start sewing (seam A/B in Fig. 15).

Stitcher

Sew the pinned seam A/B starting at the pin point with each piece. Feed through without cutting threads or lifting the presser foot. Keep both edges as even as possible.

Important: Don't stretch the bias edge.

Helpful Tip

When sewing blocks together, take it slow to line them up. Get edges even first, then sew a couple of stitches, stop your machine with the needle down and gently ease your fabric to match the next seam or edge, holding firmly, and continue sewing past that seam or edge. Stop the machine again, match the next seam, ease to fit, continue sewing. Repeat this process for each seam

---

Pinwheel

Presser

Press all seams in the same direction — whichever works best, usually toward the seamless piece.

Everyone

You now have 72 pieces. Divide the pieces equally into piles (Fig. 16).

> **Helpful Tip**
> To make neater blocks, after pressing triangle seams nip off the "dog ears" that stick out.

Presser and Cutter

Flip right over left again as in Fig. 17.

Stitcher

Keep the edges even when sewing and butt the center seam. Sew seam C/D starting at the pin point without lifting the presser foot or cutting threads.

Presser

Press all seams taking care not to stretch the bias edge. You now have 36 light blocks — all with bias edges.

Everyone

Separate the pile of dark triangles into two piles and sew into blocks following the instructions on page 33. * Measure three or four blocks and take a happy medium of these measurements. Make a note of this measurement as you will need to use it when cutting the connecting strip.

Quilt owner

Time for a decision! Are all the light blocks going in the center or all the dark? Hop to it. The layout samples on page 31 show the difference between the two layout options to help you decide which layout you want to use. Make sure your helpers know what you have in mind.

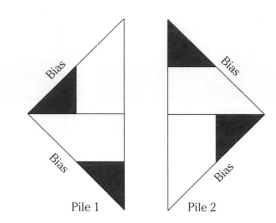

Fig. 16

> **Helpful Tip**
> When you stop sewing to line up seams, stop your machine with the needle down to keep your place.

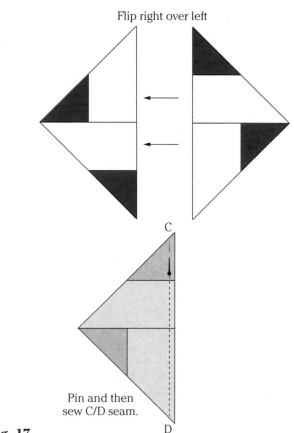

Flip right over left

Pin and then sew C/D seam.

Fig. 17

Presser and Cutter

Take the pile of blocks you are using for the center, put aside eight, and pass pairs of blocks to the Stitcher. You can turn blocks so seams are butting.

Stitcher

Sew pairs of blocks, pushing through the machine without cutting threads. Don't be upset. The only seams that match are the corner ones. You are sewing bias edges so be careful not to stretch.

Presser and Cutter

Clip threads as the pairs are completed, and return to Stitcher.

Stitcher

Sew these pairs of blocks into fours, pushing through the machine without cutting threads.

Presser and Cutter

When you have seven strips of fours, find the eight blocks you put aside and pass a fours and an extra block to the Stitcher until you've finished them all.

Stitcher

Sew one block to the end of each fours pushing through the machine without cutting threads until you have seven strips with five blocks each.

Presser

Press the seams of Row 1 to the left, Row 2 to the right, and continue, alternating the direction of the pressed seam by row.

Stitcher

Sew the rows together into a block of five blocks by seven blocks.

Presser

Press the seams of the 5 x 7 block unit flat, all seams

going in the same direction. Press the back first and then the front.

Presser and Cutter

Using the remaining blocks (all light or all dark), pass Stitcher nine blocks at a time.

Stitcher

Sew the blocks into four single columns of nine blocks each. It's quickest to sew the blocks into four sets of twos, then join those into fours, then eights, and then the ninth.

Presser

Press seams all in the same direction.

> **Helpful Tip**
> When you get to your final edge seams, it's a good idea to backstitch so the seam won't pull apart when stretching for the border and/or frame.

Cutter

Cut the connecting strip the exact width of a block before it was sewn. You will need 5 strips if you are cutting across the width of fabric, approximately 212 linear inches.

Everyone

Attach the connecting strip as directed in Chapter 3, putting the sides on first and ends last. After the connecting strip is on, add one column of 9 blocks to each side, keeping edges even and blocks directly across from each other. Add rest of blocks to top and bottom to complete the outside edge of blocks.

Add your final border(s) (see Chapter 3). Don't forget to prepare the back of your top to be ready to finish your quilt.

Trip Around the World

Trip Around the World

Inspired by "Trip Around the World," Jane C. Smith, Wells, Maine.

Menu

Simple All Season Salad, p. 116

Sweet 'n Sour Beef and
Cabbage Dinner, p. 118

Maple Nut Muffins, p. 121

My Mom's Lemon Pie, p. 124

Come along for the ride! This one is fun and easy!

Quilt Sizes

Finished size double – 81" x 103" includes 10¼" border

Finished size queen – 90" x 112" includes 14¾" border

(If these sizes are too long for your needs, you may wish to make the top border narrower.)

Size before border – 60½" x 82½"

Number of blocks – 165 (11 blocks x 15 blocks)

Finished block size – 5½"

Finished border width double – one 10¼" or one 4" and one 6¼"

Finished border width queen – one 8" and one 6¾" or one 3", one 5" and one 6¾"

Color Key

This quilt works best if you select a good contrast of colors. Usually they are numbered in these patterns from light to dark, lightest being #1, but use your imagination. Look at the layout sample and decide which squares you'd like to emphasize.

Color #1

Color #2

Color #3

Color #4

Color #5

Color #6

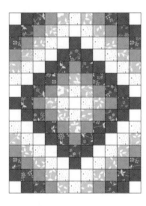

Layout Sample

Helpful Tip

To make your pressing easier, draw a straight line on your ironing board with a permanent marking pen and align the strip sets with this line.

Trip Around the World

Assembly Diagram

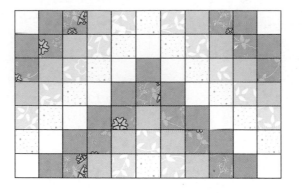

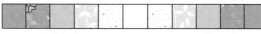

1	2	3	4	5	6	5	4	3	2	1
1	6	5	4	3	2	3	4	5	6	1
6	5	4	3	2	1	2	3	4	5	6
5	4	3	2	1	6	1	2	3	4	5
4	3	2	1	6	5	6	1	2	3	4
3	2	1	6	5	4	5	6	1	2	3
2	1	6	5	4	3	4	5	6	1	2
1	6	5	4	3	2	3	4	5	6	1

Division Strip

6	5	4	3	2	1	2	3	4	5	6

38

Fabric Requirements (44/45" fabric)

Colors #1 – #6 – 1 yard each					
	Double			**Queen**	
One Border	10¼"	2¾ yards			
Two Borders or {	4"	2 yards	{	8"	2 yards
&	6¼"	2 yards	&	6¾"	2 yards
Three Borders	—	—		3"	1 yard
	—	—	or {	5"	1½ yards
			&	6¾"	2¼ yards
Binding	⅞ yard			1 yard	
Backing	6⅛ yards			8 yards	

Putting the team to work

Stitcher

Adjust the machine to a shorter than average stitch length because you will to be cutting across seams. Try a seam on scrap fabric to get a ¼" seam and fill two or three bobbins with neutral thread.

Cutter

If you have made some of the other quilts in this book, you must stop and rethink! Strips will be cut with the lengthwise grain of fabric this time so fold your fabric to cut strips along the short side of the fabric (Fig. 18). Fold cut edge to cut edge, cut off one selvage, and cut your strips from this same side. Cut 2 strips from Color #1 and 1 strip from Colors #2 – 6, each 6" wide.

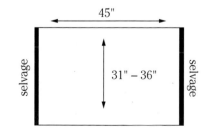

Fig. 18

Presser

Give strips to the Stitcher in the order shown in Fig. 19, p. 40. For example, for Strip set 1, give the strips to the Stitcher in 1, 6, 5, 4, 3, 2, 1 order. Notice: The six strip sets have their own distinctive patterns.

Cutter

Continue cutting 6" strips until you have seven strips of each color.

Stitcher

Sew the strips together in the order given to you by the Presser. You'll be making 6 strip sets, each one different.

Presser

On wrong side, press seams flat as sewn, then lightly press each seam toward darkest fabric. Or, if you desire, press the seams in Strip set 1 in one direction and Strip set 2 in the other, depending on how they look on the right side. Turn to the right side and press each set to the fullest width, keeping the set as straight as possible.

Cutter

Cut across each strip set, aligning the ruler with the

> **Helpful Tip**
> If you like, you can use the same fabric in several places. Determine the extra yardage before you purchase your fabric, and label each fabric piece with the color numbers before you begin.

seams as shown in Fig. 20. First trim off the uneven edge, then cut four strips from each set, again cutting strip 6" wide. (After you have cut a few pieces, realign the ruler to make sure your cuts remain perfect.) Make a pile of the strips from each set and label them to avoid confusion (Set 1, Set 2, etc.).

Presser

Lay out the pieced strips as illustrated in assembly diagram, p. 38, and give these to the Stitcher in order. You will need 11 pieced strips to make the top half of the quilt.

Stitcher

Sew the 11 pieced strips together in the order they are handed to you and match the block corners as closely as possible.

Presser

Lay out another set of pieced strips as illustrated in assembly diagram, p. 38. Give the set to the Stitcher in order. These will be the 11 pieced strips for the bottom half of the quilt.

Stitcher

Sew the 11 pieced strips together in the order they are handed to you, matching the block corners as closely as possible.

Everyone

Before putting the top and bottom halves together, make up your division strip of blocks by removing a few seams and rearranging blocks of your leftover pieced strips in the order in diagram on page 38.

Presser and Cutter

Referring to the assembly diagram, p. 38, lay out the top and bottom of the quilt together with the division strip. Be certain to turn the bottom section around so it is oriented properly. Hand these sections to the Stitcher.

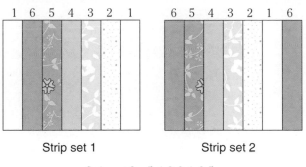

Strip set 3 – 5, 4, 3, 2, 1, 6, 5
Strip set 4 – 4, 3, 2, 1, 6, 5, 4
Strip set 5 – 3, 2, 1, 6, 5, 4, 3
Strip set 6 – 2, 1, 6, 5, 4, 3, 2

Fig. 19

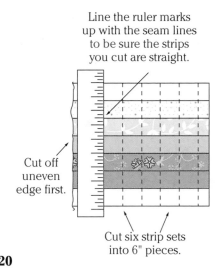

Line the ruler marks up with the seam lines to be sure the strips you cut are straight.

Cut off uneven edge first.

Cut six strip sets into 6" pieces.

Fig. 20

Stitcher

Sew three sections together across the quilt. Match the block corners as closely as possible.

Presser

Press seams carefully.

Now your quilt is ready for the border (see Chapter 3). Don't forget to prepare the backing of your quilt to be ready to finish your quilt.

Log Cabin

Blocks in this quilt can be arranged in a multitude of ways, creating a stunningly different quilt each time.

Log Cabin

Menu

Ham and Biscuit Dinner, p. 117.

Nutty Fruit Salad, p. 116

Rhubarb Berry Cobbler, p. 125

Block Sample

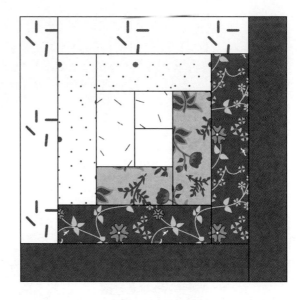

Quilt Sizes

Finished size double with 20 blocks – 81" x 95" includes 12½" border

Finished size queen with 20 blocks – 90" x 104" includes 17" border

Finished size double with 24 blocks – 81" x 109" includes 12½" border

Finished size queen with 24 blocks – 90" x 118" includes 17" border

Size before border with 20 blocks – 56" x 70"

Size before border with 24 blocks – 56" x 84" (See page 43 for layouts possible when choosing a 20 or 24 block quilt)

Finished block size – 14"

Finished border width double – one 12½" or one 3", one 4" and one 5½"

Finished border width queen – one 17" or one 4", one 5½", and one 7½"

Color Key

The traditional Log Cabin was made with light colors in one corner of the block and dark in the opposite corner, often with a red or yellow center representing the fire in the hearth or the light in the window. For your fabric selection, select contrasting colors, light and dark, or two different colors of varying intensities.

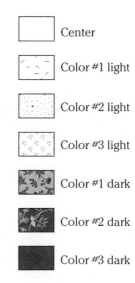

Center

Color #1 light

Color #2 light

Color #3 light

Color #1 dark

Color #2 dark

Color #3 dark

Layout Samples

The layouts can also be used for the Amish Shadow quilt. Experiment to create a layout that is perfect for you.

Note: Choosing 20 blocks will limit your choice of the final quilt design. Choosing 24 blocks will make an extra long quilt but will give you more flexibility in layout design. If you prefer a shorter quilt but want to use 24 blocks, you can eliminate all or some of the top border.

With 20 blocks

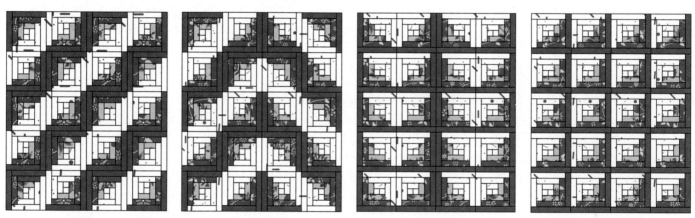

With 24 blocks

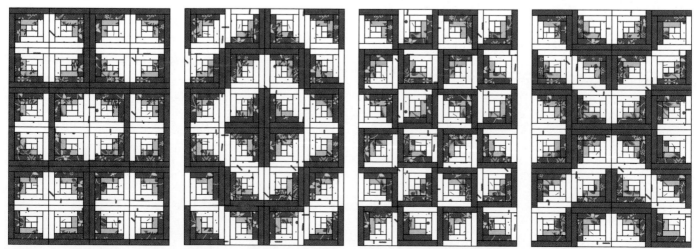

Log Cabin

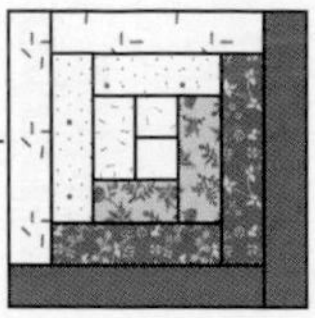

Fabric Requirements: (44/45" fabric)

	20 blocks	24 blocks
Center	¼ yard	¼ yard
#1 Light	½ yard	½ yard
#2 Light	¾ yard	1 yard
#3 Light	1¼ yards	1½ yards
#1 Dark	⅔ yard	¾ yard
#2 Dark	1 yard	1¼ yards
#3 Dark	1½ yards	1¾ yards

	Width	20 blocks	24 blocks
Double			
1 Border	12½"	3½ yards	3½ yards
3 Borders	3"	1 yard	1 yard
or	4"	1¼ yards	1⅓ yards
	5½"	1⅝ yards	1¾ yards
Queen			
1 Border	17"	4½ yards	5½ yards
3 Borders	4"	1¼ yards	1¼ yards
or	5½"	1⅝ yards	1⅔ yards
	7½"	2⅓ yards	2½ yards
Back and Binding			
Double Back		5¾ yards	6⅓ yards
Double Binding		¾ yards	⅞ yards
Queen Back		8 yards	8 yards
Queen Binding		⅞ yards	1 yard

Quilt top owner

Determine which quilt layout you want to use. Be sure to make 24 blocks if you want to use one of the designs on page 43 that needs 24! Be sure your friends know what layout you are planning to use so there isn't any confusion when things start cooking!

Putting the team to work

Stitcher

Adjust the machine to a shorter than average stitch length because you will be cutting across seams. Try a seam on scrap fabric to get a ¼" seam and fill two or three bobbins with neutral thread.

Cutter

Fold your fabric and even the raw edges. Then, cut 2 strips of Center fabric and 2 strips of Color #1 Light, each 2½" wide across width of fabric.

Presser

Give strips to the Stitcher.

Stitcher

Sew a Color #1 strip to the Center strip, right sides together along one long, side and pass to the Presser. Repeat with the second set of strips.

Presser

Lay the sewn strip set on the pressing table and press flat. Now open the set so the strips lie side by side. Lightly, on the wrong side of fabric, press seam away from Center strip. Turn to the right side and press to the fullest width, keeping the set as straight as possible.

Cutter

Continue cutting the rest of the strips 2½" wide in the following order:

	20 blocks	24 blocks
#1 Light	3 more	3 more
#1 Dark	6	6
#2 Light	8	9
#2 Dark	10	12
#3 Light	12	14
#3 Dark	14	16

Don't be concerned if you need to cut more later, fabrics vary.

Presser

As soon as you have one strip set pressed, ask the Cutter to do the next step or, if possible, do the next step yourself to keep things moving along.

Cutter (or Presser)

Cut the selvage off the strip set. Cut 20 or 24 rectangular pieces, each 2½" wide from this set (see Fig. 21, p. 46). Cut an extra so the owner can have an extra block for posterity! (After you have cut a few pieces, realign the ruler so you do not cut crooked pieces.)

Presser

As soon as you (or the Cutter) have a few rectangles cut, give these to the Stitcher with another 2½" strip Color #1 Light. (Take a minute to recount your pieces.) Go ahead and use whatever is left of the first strip.

Stitcher

Lay another #1 Light strip on the machine, right side up. Lay the pieced rectangle on top of it, right side down, with the Center fabric toward you and the #1 Light fabric up and away from you. Drop it below the selvage and sew on the right-hand edge. When you are close to the end of the rectangle, stop and add a second rectangle, butting, but not overlapping, the first one. Continue until all 20 (24) are on the strip (Fig. 22, p. 46).

Log Cabin

Presser

Take the strips from the Stitcher as each strip is filled with the pieced rectangles. With the uncut strip on the bottom, press flat, as sewn.

Cutter

Cut the bottom strip between the pieces. If the Stitcher has done her job well, only one cut will have to be made between each piece. If a space has been left between the rectangles, two cuts must be made to cut the space out of the bottom strip. Suggest kindly that the Stitcher try to butt but not overlap the pieces (Fig. 23).

Presser

Press as before, seam away from the center. Give the cut pieces to the Stitcher upside down with the long #1 Light portion away from her. Also be sure she has a #1 Dark strip to continue.

Stitcher

Changing color as before, lay a #1 Dark strip right side up on the machine. Skipping the selvage, lay the pieced section on top right side down, with the last piece that you added up and away from you. Drop below the selvage and sew on the right-hand edge. When you are near the end of the pieced section, stop and add a second pieced section, butting, but not overlapping, the first one. Continue until all 20 (24) are on a strip (Fig. 24).

Presser

Take the strips from the Stitcher as each strip is filled with the pieced squares. With the uncut strip on the bottom, press flat.

Cutter

Cut the bottom strip between the pieces. Again, if there is a space between the rectangles, you must make two cuts to cut the space out of the bottom

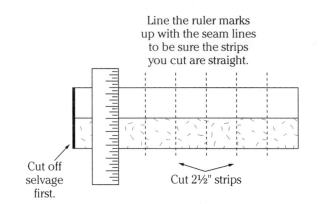

Line the ruler marks up with the seam lines to be sure the strips you cut are straight.

Cut off selvage first.

Cut 2½" strips

Fig. 21

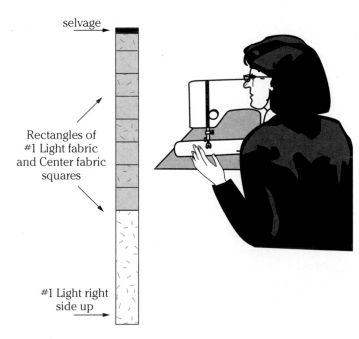

selvage

Rectangles of #1 Light fabric and Center fabric squares

#1 Light right side up

Fig. 22

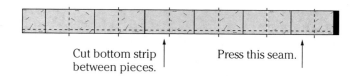

Cut bottom strip between pieces.   Press this seam.

Fig. 23

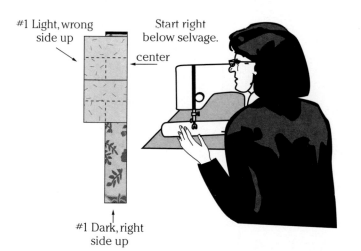

#1 Light, wrong side up

Start right below selvage.

center

#1 Dark, right side up

Fig. 24

strip. (If this is the case, you might mention it again to the Stitcher.)

Presser
Press as before, seam away from the center.

Everyone
Continue in the same manner, sewing the pieced sections to the next color strip. Remember you always add two sections of each color. Once you have two #1 Light and two #1 Dark strips on, it is easy! Always add the light strip to the light side and the dark strip to the dark side. As you look at the right side, you are always going counterclockwise.

When all blocks are complete, lay them out in the chosen pattern. Refer to page 43 for suggestions.

Presser and Cutter
Starting with the first two columns, flip block #2 over block #1 and pin the side to be sewn. Repeat with #4 over #3, #6 over #5, #8 over #7, #10 over #9 (and #22 over #21). Hand the pieces to be sewn to the Stitcher (Figs. 25 and 26, p. 48).

Stitcher
Sew the pinned pairs together, trying to keep the edges even. Ease as needed and match seams when they come together. Feed pieces through the machine without cutting the thread between blocks.

Presser and Cutter
Take these back to the table and lay them in place.

Everyone
Repeat with the next two columns, 12 over 11, etc. Lay the blocks down with the first batch.

Log Cabin

Presser and Cutter

Flip 11 – 12 over 1 – 2 and 13 – 14 over 3 – 4, etc. Give these to the Stitcher, making sure you remember which blocks are which! Pinning the seam to be sewn with the point of the pin marking where the stitcher should start sewing will help avoid confusion.

Stitcher

Try to keep the edges even as you sew the pairs into fours, easing as needed. Match seams when they come together and feed pieces through machine without cutting the thread between blocks.

Presser

You now have four blocks across. You may press these but be sure you know which block is #1. Press all seams toward #1 in the first row and all seams toward #14 in the second row, all seams toward #5 in the third row, all seams toward #18 in the fourth row, all seams toward #9 in the fifth row (and all seams toward #24 in the sixth row if necessary).

Presser and Cutter

Hand the rows to the Stitcher in order.

Stitcher

Sew the rows together, matching seams as closely as possible.

You're ready for the border. Refer to Chapter 3 for border instructions. Good job! Don't forget to prepare the backing of your quilt.

	Columns		
1	2	3	4
1	2	11	12
3	4	13	14
5	6	15	16
7	8	17	18
9	10	19	20
21	22	23	24

Fig. 25

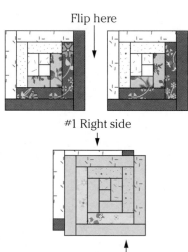

Flip here

#1 Right side

#2 Wrong side

Fig. 26

Split Rail or Knot

This quilt was inspired by Strip Rail quilt by Trudie Hughes.

More Template Free Quilting, That Patchwork Place, 1987

Split Rail or Knot

Waldorf Salad, p. 117

Seedy Baked Chicken, p. 118

Refrigerator Bran Muffins, p. 121

Brownie (easier than) Pie, p. 122

Menu

You'll learn a new trick with this quilt. Try for really consistent seams and an extra special pressing job.

Quilt Sizes

Finished size double – 81" x 98" includes 6½" border

Finished size queen – 90" x 107" includes 11" border

Size before border – 68" x 85"

Number of blocks – 80 (8 blocks x 10 blocks)

Finished block size – 8½"

Finished border width double – one 6½"

Finished border width queen – one 11" or one 6½" and one 4½"

Block Samples

You will end up with two different blocks. We'll call one a light block and one a dark.

Dark Block

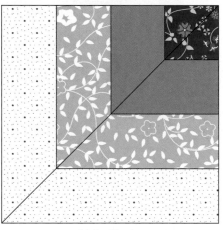

Light Block

Color Key

Color #1   Color #2   Color #3   Color #4

50

Layout Samples

Quilt top owner

Determine which of the three layouts you would like to use. Possible layouts are shown in the diagrams below. Clue your partners in on your decision to avoid chaos later.

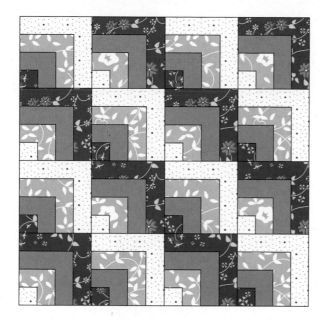

Split Rail

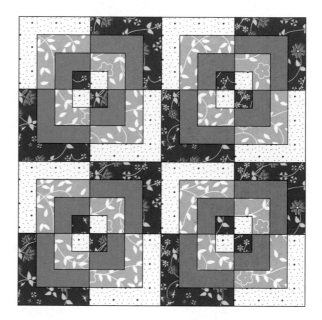

Four-Patch Knot

Knot

Split Rail or Knot

Fabric Requirements (44/45" fabric)

Colors #1 – #4: 1¾ yards each				
	Double		**Queen**	
One Border	6½"	1¾ yards	11"	3⅛ yards
Two Borders	—	—	or { 6½"	1¾ yards
	—	—	4½"	1½ yards
Binding	¾ yard		⅞ yard	
Backing	5⅞ yards		8 yards	

Putting the team to work

Stitcher

Adjust machine to a shorter than average stitch length because you will be cutting across seams. Try a seam on scrap fabric to get a ¼" seam and fill two or three bobbins with neutral thread.

Cutter

Fold your fabric and even up the raw edges (see Chapter 2). Then, cut one strip from each of Colors #1, 2, 3, and 4, each 2¾" wide across width of fabric.

Presser

Give strips to Stitcher in order (Fig. 27).

Stitcher

Make a strip set by sewing the long edges together as shown in Fig. 27. You'll be making 20 identical strip sets.

Cutter

Cut 19 more strips of each color, 2¾" wide across the width of the fabric. Be sure to have some of each fabric ready so you don't hold up the Stitcher.

Presser

Take two strip sets at once to the pressing table. On the wrong side, lightly press the seams in one set

1 2 3 4

Fig. 27

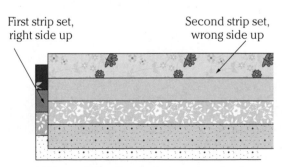

First strip set, right side up

Second strip set, wrong side up

Align carefully, directly on top of each other.

Fig. 28

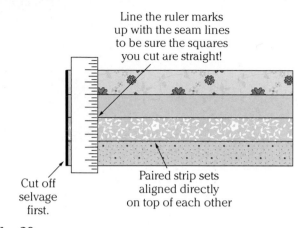

Line the ruler marks up with the seam lines to be sure the squares you cut are straight!

Cut off selvage first.

Paired strip sets aligned directly on top of each other

Fig. 29

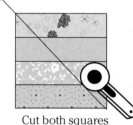

Cut both squares together with one cut.

Fig. 30

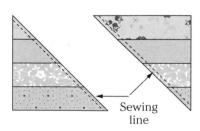

Sewing line

Fig. 31

toward Color #1 and the other toward Color #4. Turn to the right side, keeping seams as pressed. Press each set to the fullest width, keeping it as straight as possible. Pass these two pressed sets to the Cutter and do all 10 pairs the same way, keeping pairs together.

Cutter

Measure the width of the strip set — should be approximately 9½". You will be cutting squares this measurement. Lay out one set right side up. Put second set from that pair directly on top, right sides together with seams butting together and edges exactly even (see Fig. 28).

From the end you are cutting, cut off selvage edges . Be sure to keep seams aligned as you cut squares. You should get four squares from each strip set. (After you have cut a few pieces, realign the ruler.) Be extremely careful to keep both squares together, especially if you move them from place to place (Fig. 29).

Cut each pair of squares with one diagonal cut. Be sure to cut the same diagonal each time, always keeping the same strip toward you (Fig. 30).

Presser

Hand the triangle pairs to the Stitcher, being careful not to let them slip.

Stitcher

Sew the diagonal edges together, being careful not to stretch bias (Fig. 31).

Presser

Take sewn triangles from the Stitcher as she finishes the seams. Press the seams in one direction, keeping the blocks as square as possible.

Split Rail or Knot

Cutter

Keep blocks in two piles, light and dark (Fig. 32).

Everyone

Lay out the blocks according to the pattern you have chosen. You will make 4 sets of twos, then fours, then eights for each row as explained below.

Presser and Cutter

Starting with the first two columns, flip block #2 over block #1 and pin the side you want sewn. Repeat with #4 over #3, #6 over #5, and so on (Figs. 33 and 34).

Stitcher

Keep the edges even, easing as needed. Match seams when they come together, and feed pieces through the machine without cutting the thread between blocks.

Presser and Cutter

Take back to the table and lay in place.

Everyone

Repeat with the next two columns, 22 over 21, and so on. Then repeat with the 5th and 6th columns and the 7th and 8th columns. Lay the blocks down with the first batch.

Presser and Cutter

Now make the first two columns of twos into fours. Flip 21 – 22 over 1 – 2 and 23 – 24 over 3 – 4, etc. Give these to the Stitcher, making sure you remember which blocks are which, and she knows which seam to sew!

Helpful Tip

When pressing the seams in the final rows of your quilt, before sewing all the rows together it is easier on the Stitcher if you will alternate the direction you press your seams. However, if this quilt is to be hand quilted, the quilter might prefer all seams going the same direction.

Finished squares, pressed full
and kept in two separate piles.

Fig. 32

Columns							
1	2	3	4	5	6	7	8
1	2	21	22	41	42	61	62
3	4	23	24	43	44	63	64
5	6	25	26	45	46	65	66
7	8	27	28	47	48	67	68
9	10	29	30	49	50	69	70
11	12	31	32	51	52	71	72
13	14	33	34	53	54	73	74
15	16	35	36	55	56	75	76
17	18	37	38	57	58	77	78
19	20	39	40	59	60	79	80

Fig. 33

Stitcher

Keep the edges even, easing as needed. Match seams when they come together and feed pieces through the machine without cutting the thread between blocks.

Everyone

Continue with the next two column of twos (put 61 – 62 over 41 – 42, etc.) and sew. You will now have 20 fours.

Presser and Cutter

Working one row at a time, flip one fours (41 – 42 – 61 – 62) over the other fours (1 – 2 – 21 – 22). Give

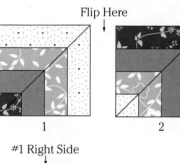

Flip Here

1   2

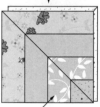

#1 Right Side

Align directly on top of each other and pin seam to be sewn.

#2 Wrong Side

Fig. 34

to the Stitcher and continue with the rest of the rows, making sure you remember which blocks are being stitched.

Stitcher

Sew the fours into eights. Keep edges even, easing as needed. Match seams when they come together and feed pieces through the machine without cutting the thread.

Presser

Press the seams in each row as it is stitched together, first row to the left, second to the right, alternating by row. Then press flat on the right side. Be careful to keep the rows in the correct order.

Everyone

Now you have 10 rows of eight blocks each.

Cutter

Hand the first two pressed rows to the Stitcher. As the seams are finished, hand the Stitcher each of the remaining rows in order.

Stitcher

Sew the rows together carefully, matching the corners of the blocks as closely as possible.

Presser

Press all seams carefully in one direction.

Fantastic! Now your quilt top is ready for the border. Refer to Chapter 3 for instructions on borders. Don't forget to prepare your quilt backing.

Amish Shadow

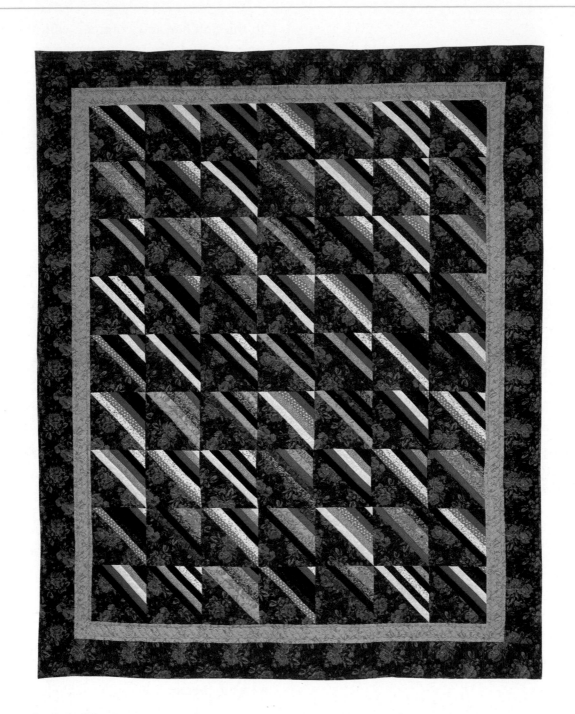

Amish Shadow

This is a traditional Amish pattern which is also called Roman Stripe.

Menu

Crisp Noodle Cabbage Salad, p. 116

Leftover Turkey/Broccoli Bake, p. 118

Cranberry Sauce

Betty's Lemon Bread, p. 119

Chilled Blueberry Banana Pie, p. 123

Quilt Sizes

Finished size double – 81" x 102" includes 3¾"
  border

Finished size queen – 90" x 111" includes 8¼"
  border (If these finished sizes are too long, you
  can make just 56 blocks, 7 blocks x 8 blocks)

Size before border – 73½" x 94½"

Number of blocks – 63 (7 blocks x 9 blocks)

Finished block size – 10½"

Finished border width double – one 3¾"

Finished border width queen – one 8¼" or one
  3¼" and one 5"

Block Sample

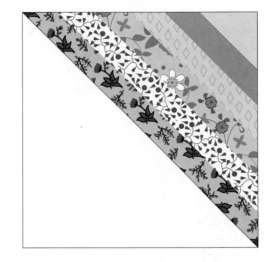

*No rules here! You can use only six fabrics or as
many as you want. You can place them randomly or
in the same sequence. You can use the traditional
plains or go as wild as you like. The unpieced side of
the block is traditionally black, but a large print
removes it from the realm of the Amish and gives it a
whole new life! Check out the samples that follow for
some inspiration.*

Color Key

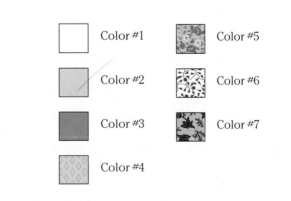

Color #1   Color #5

Color #2   Color #6

Color #3   Color #7

Color #4

Amish Shadow

Layout Samples

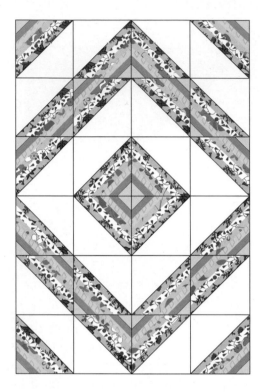

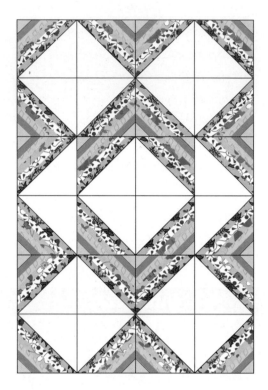

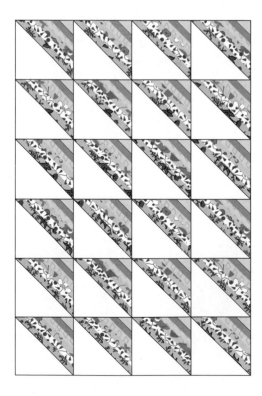

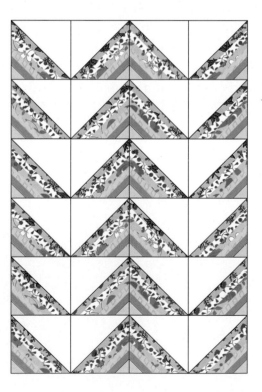

Fabric Requirements (44/45" fabric)

Plain side color – 3¾ yards (Note: You may have 1 yard left for border or binding. The size of your blocks determines the amount required.)

Pieced side colors – 6 yards total (You may use as many different colors as you like. For the sake of discussion, we're using just six in these instructions.)

	Double		Queen	
One Border	3¾"	1½ yards	8¼"	3 yards
Two Borders	—	—	or { 3¼"	1¼ yards
	—	—	5"	1⅞ yards
Binding	⅞ yard		1 yard	
Backing	6 yards		8 yards	

Quilt top owner

Determine the fabric order for the pieced side of the blocks. Make sure it's clear to your coworkers so the piecing will not be interrupted for decision making and discussion. (Make a sample and pin it up for reference.)

Putting the team to work

Stitcher

Adjust the machine to a shorter than average stitch length because you will be cutting across seams. Try a seam on scrap fabric to get a ¼" seam and fill two or three bobbins with a neutral thread.

Cutter

Fold your fabric and even up the raw edges, then cut one strip of each fabric to be used in the pieced side of the blocks 1¾" wide across the width of the fabric. Continue cutting the next strips until you have cut enough for at least 13 strip sets, 78 strips divided among the fabrics. (If you are using six colors, 13 of each color are needed.) As soon as you know how many triangles each strip set yields, you

can cut more if necessary. If there are five per set, you will have enough.

Presser

Give the strips to the Stitcher in the predetermined order. As soon as a set of six is sewn together, lightly press the seams to one side, or, if necessary, press any that shadow through fabrics toward the darker of the two.

Turn to the right side and press the strip set to the fullest width, keeping the set as straight as possible.

Stitcher

Take the first strip and fold one corner at a 45° angle (Fig. 35). Unfold and lay strip #2 onto #1 (right sides together) placing the end of strip #2 ¼" above the lower end of your fold line. Measure how far you have indented. It should be about 1¼".

Continue with strips 3, 4, 5, and 6, indenting each the same as the first. When sewn, they should look like Fig. 36. You will be making from 13 to 16 strip sets like this.

Amish Shadow

Cutter

Using a square or triangle ruler (or make a template from template plastic), place the ruler on the top of the strip set using the lines on the ruler or masking tape to keep it aligned with seam lines. Flipping the ruler, cut into triangles (Fig. 37). Count these and divide this number into 63 to get the total number of sets needed. As you cut the triangles, realign your ruler regularly to be certain you are not cutting crooked.

When you get a minute, cut more strips if needed. If there are only four triangles per set, 18 more strips will be needed. If there are less than 4, the Stitcher has made the seams too small! Believe it or not, the wider the seams, the more triangles per set.

For the plain side of the blocks, measure line A/B (Fig. 38) on a few pieced blocks, being careful not to stretch. (It is cut on the bias and may stretch.)

Take the average measurement and cut 32 squares this size (about 10½") from your plain fabric. You may get four across your fabric. If not, see Fig. 39.

Cut *along* the selvage instead of across to get the most from your fabric. Then cut each square from corner to corner to make 63 triangles (Fig. 40).

Presser and Cutter

Hand the Stitcher a plain triangle and a pieced triangle. Continue handing these units to her until all the blocks are completed.

Stitcher

Sew the blocks together carefully without lifting the presser foot. Have your helpers pass them to the Presser as you sew. Be especially careful to keep both edges even. The bias would love to stretch.

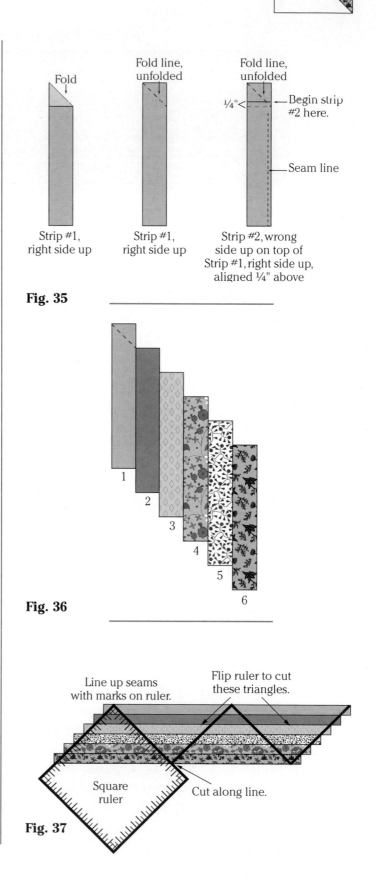

Fold line, unfolded

Fold line, unfolded

Fold

¼" — Begin strip #2 here.

— Seam line

Strip #1, right side up

Strip #1, right side up

Strip #2, wrong side up on top of Strip #1, right side up, aligned ¼" above

Fig. 35

1

2

3

4

5

6

Fig. 36

Line up seams with marks on ruler.

Flip ruler to cut these triangles.

Square ruler

Cut along line.

Fig. 37

Amish Shadow

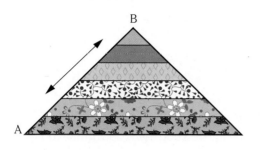

Fig. 38

Leave long strip along side to use in border.

Cut triangles from squares.

Fig. 39

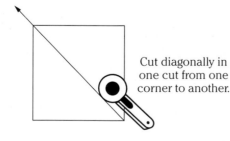

Cut diagonally in one cut from one corner to another.

Fig. 40

Presser

Lightly press seams to one side, or, if necessary, press any that shadow through toward the darker of the two. Turn to right side and press block to fullest width, keeping it as straight as possible. In order to avoid stretching the bias edges, press your seams by lifting the iron, repositioning it, and placing it down rather than sliding it along. Sometimes sliding the iron will stretch the bias edge.

Everyone

When all the blocks are made, lay them out in the order of the traditional layout as shown on page 58, one of the layouts from the Log Cabin on page 43, or in another layout you design.

> **Helpful Tip**
> To make blocks neater after pressing triangle seams, nip off ears that stick out.

If you are following the traditional pattern:

Presser and Cutter

Before laying the blocks out, remove nine and set them aside. Divide the rest of the blocks into two piles, both oriented the same way. Take a block from each pile and give these to the Stitcher. Continue to hand the blocks two at a time, keeping them properly oriented.

Stitcher

Keeping the blocks oriented the same way, flip one block over the other and sew the right-hand seam. Sew pairs without lifting the presser foot. When you have nine pairs sewn together, hand them to the Presser.

Presser and Cutter

Snip threads and lay out nine pairs down and three across. Give the pairs to the Stitcher to be stitched

Amish Shadow

into fours and then pass the last pairs to make them into sixes.

Stitcher

Sew the pairs into fours without lifting the presser foot, then add the third row of pairs to make sixes in the same manner.

Presser and Cutter

Snip the threads between the nine sixes. From the nine blocks you set aside, add one to each of the sixes.

Presser

When completed, press the seams in the first row to the left, the seams in the second row to the right, and so on.

Now go to the **For All Layouts** section (page 63).

If you choose a non-traditional pattern:

Everyone

Lay out the blocks in the pattern you like best.

Presser and Cutter

Starting with the first two columns of blocks, flip the second column of blocks over their first column counterparts (that is, Block #2 over Block #1, #4 over #3, #6 over #5, etc.) and put a pin in the side to be sewn (Figs. 41 and 42).

> **Helpful Tip**
>
> It's a good idea to make a color guide of your fabrics so there is no confusion. Just cut a small sample along a selvage edge and tape it beside your color numbers in sequence.

Stitcher

Try to keep the edges even, easing as needed. Feed pieces through the machine without cutting the thread between blocks.

Presser and Cutter

Take these back to the table and lay them in place.

Everyone

Repeat with the next two columns, 20 over 19, etc. Then repeat with the 5th and 6th columns. Lay the blocks down with the first batch.

Presser and Cutter

Now that you have six sets of twos (and one extra block) in each row, join your twos to make fours. Flip 19 – 20 over 1 – 2 and 21 – 22 over 3 – 4 and so on. Give to Stitcher, making sure you remember which blocks are which.

Stitcher

Sew the twos into fours as they are handed to you. Try to keep the edges even, easing as needed and matching seams when they come together. Feed pieces through the machine without cutting the thread between blocks.

Everyone

Add the next column of twos to the fours (that is, put 37 – 38 over 1 – 2 – 19 – 20) and sew. You will now have nine units of six.

Presser and Cutter

Give the Stitcher the first sixes and the final block on that row. Follow with the second sixes and the final block on that row. Continue through all the rows.

Stitcher

Sew the final block on the row and hand it back to the Presser or Cutter.

Columns

1	2	3	4	5	6	7
1	2	19	20	37	38	55
3	4	21	22	39	40	56
5	6	23	24	41	42	57
7	8	25	26	43	44	58
9	10	27	28	45	46	59
11	12	29	30	47	48	60
13	14	31	32	49	50	61
15	16	33	34	51	52	62
17	18	35	36	53	54	63

Fig. 41

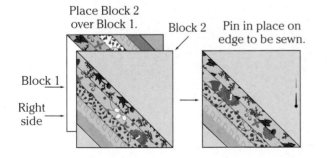

Place Block 2 over Block 1. Block 2 Pin in place on edge to be sewn. Block 1 Right side

Fig. 42

For All Layouts

Presser

You now have seven blocks across. You can press but be sure you know which block is #1 (you could put a pin in the top left-hand corner as a reminder). Press all seams to the left in the first row, all seams to the right in the second row, all seams to the left in the third row, and continue alternating the direction of each pressed seam by row. This makes it easier on the Stitcher. However, if this quilt is to be hand quilted, the quilter might prefer all the seams going in the same direction.

Presser and Cutter

Give rows to the Stitcher in order.

Stitcher

Sew all nine rows together across the quilt. Match the block corners as closely as possible.

Presser

Press seams carefully.

Now your quilt is ready for the border, see Chapter 3 for instructions. Don't forget to prepare the backing for finishing.

Pieces of Eight

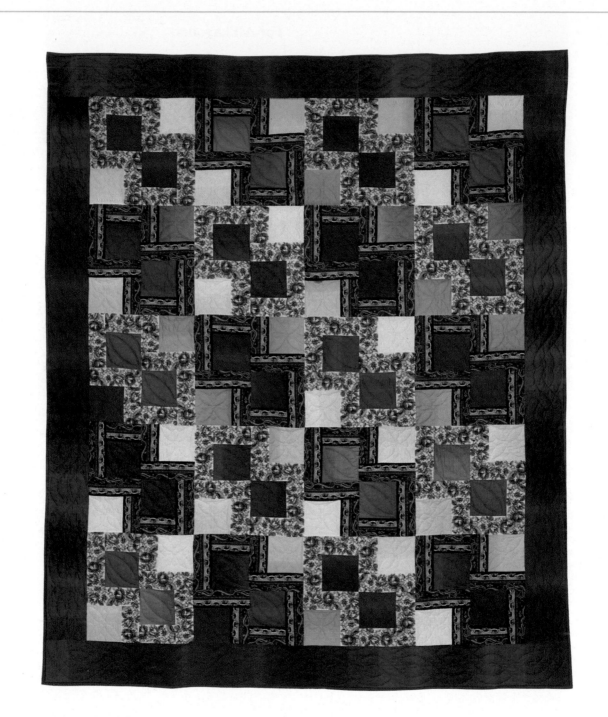

Pieces of Eight

Inspired by "Patience," designed by Debra Wagner.

Quick and Easy Quilting, Spring 1991, House of White Birches, Berne, Indiana

Menu

Glazed Fruit Cup, p. 116

Zesty Spaghetti Salad, p. 119

Easy Sticky Buns, p. 120

Lona's Lemon Angel Dessert, p. 123

This is one of the easiest quilts to make, but don't let that fact mesmerize you. It takes awhile to get 80 blocks sewn together!

Quilt Sizes

Finished size double – 81" x 99" includes a 4½" border

Finished size queen – 90" x 108" includes a 9" border

Size before border – 72" x 90"

Number of blocks – 80 (8 blocks by 10 blocks)

Finished block size – 9"

Finished border width double – one 4½"

Finished border width queen – one 9" or one 5½" and one 3½"

Block Samples

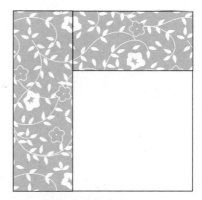

Block A

Block B

Color Key

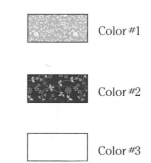

(Color #3 may be a number of different colors)

Pieces of Eight

Layout Samples

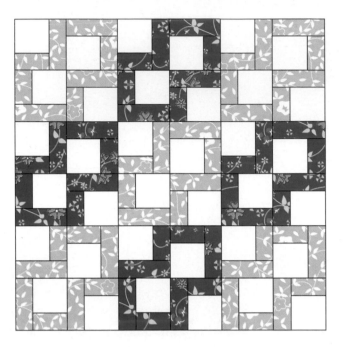

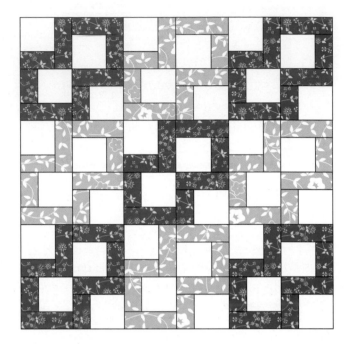

This layout features more light figure 8's than dark ones, all going in the same diagonal direction.

In this layout, there are more dark 8's than light 8's, still going in the same direction.

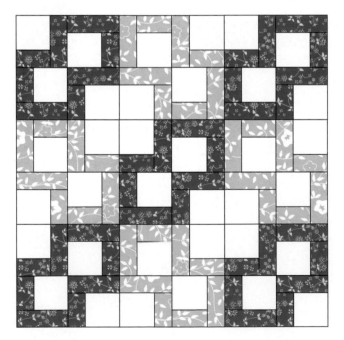

This layout has light figure 8's along one diagonal and dark figure 8's along the opposite diagonal.

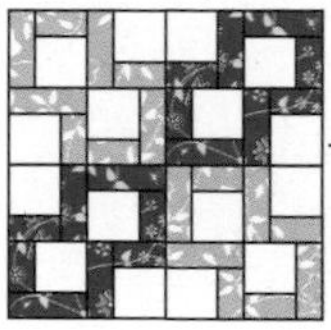

Fabric Requirements (44/45" fabric)

Color #1: 1⅞ yards, or if cutting striped fabric, 670 linear inches
Color #2: 1⅞ yards, or if cutting striped fabric, 670 linear inches
Color #3: 3 yards total divided into as many colors as wanted.

	Double		Queen	
One border	4½"	1½ yards	9"	2¾ yards
Two borders	—	—	or { 5½"	1¾ yards
	—	—	3½"	1¼ yards
Binding	¾ yard		⅞ yard	
Backing	5⅞ yards		8 yards	

Helpful Tip

To determine the amount of striped fabric needed, count the number of stripe repeats across the chosen fabric. Divide the required linear inches (670) by the number of repeats; that total is divided by 36 to determine the yardage required.

Example: 670 linear inches ÷ 8 repeats = 83.75" needed
83.75" ÷ 36 = 2.32 yds. required

You may choose to use one fabric or many different ones. If you are working in a group, and using a striped fabric, cut the striped fabric before you get together. Fabric must be unfolded and cut with scissors or a rotary cutter, and the cutting would take up too much of the group's valuable time.

Shaded fabrics and stripes can add pizazz to your quilt. This Pieces of Eight quilt was made using the shaded fabrics in the picture on page 12.

Quilt top owner

Determine the layout you wish to use and inform your teammates. In the three layouts for Pieces of Eight, the same squares were used for all layouts — simply rearranged.

Stitcher

Adjust the machine to a shorter than average stitch length because we are going to be cutting across seams. Try a seam on scrap fabric to get a ¼" seam, and fill two or three bobbins with neutral thread.

Cutter

Fold your fabric and even up the raw edges. Then, cut a strip of Color #1 3½" wide across the width of the fabric. Cut a strip of Color #3 6½" wide across the width of the fabric. Then continue cutting the following in an order that keeps the Stitcher hopping:

Color #	Cut Size	# of Strips
1	3½"	16
2	3½"	16
3	6½"	14*

*distributed evenly among all fabrics included in Color #3.

Presser

Give the first two strips of Color #1 and Color #3 to the Stitcher.

Pieces of Eight

Stitcher

With the narrow strip on the machine, sew on a wide strip, right sides together. Pass to the Presser.

Presser

As the Cutter cuts the rest of the 14 wide strips, sort them into two piles, dividing the different colors equally between them. Put one pile aside to use in making Block B. Give the Stitcher a wide strip from the remaining pile along with a strip of Color #1 until you have completed seven strip sets.

Stitcher

Sew the remaining strips until you have completed seven (Fig. 43). As you finish them, pass the strip sets to the Presser.

Presser

Press the seams flat, then toward the narrow strip. Press each strip set to the fullest width, keeping the rectangle as straight as possible.

Cutter

Align your ruler with the seams and cut off the selvage first, then cut the set into 6½" pieces (Fig. 44). (After you have cut a few pieces, realign the ruler to make sure the cuts are straight.)

Stitcher

Lay another strip of Color #1 on the machine. Sew the pieced sections onto it, with the square toward you and the narrow strip up and away from you, right sides together. The narrow piece should go through the machine first. Stitch with the squares meeting, but not overlapping, without lifting the presser foot until you come to the end of your strip (Fig. 45).

Presser

Lay strip set on the pressing table and press the seam flat as sewn. Then press the set open to the

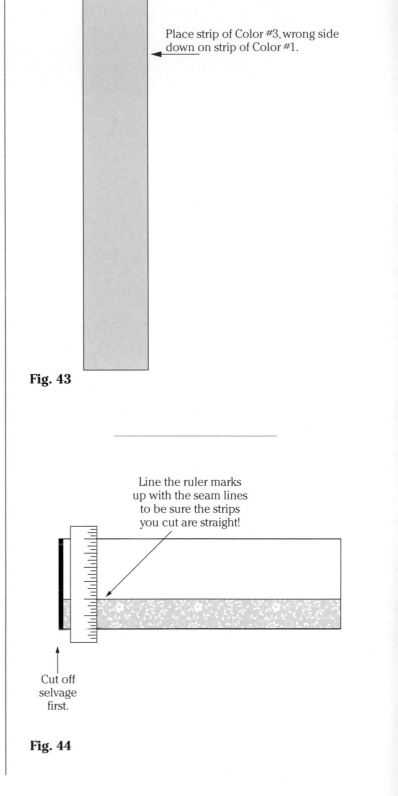

Start below selvage

Place strip of Color #3, wrong side down on strip of Color #1.

Fig. 43

Line the ruler marks up with the seam lines to be sure the strips you cut are straight!

Cut off selvage first.

Fig. 44

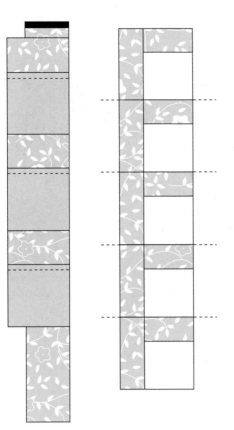

Fig. 45   **Fig. 46**

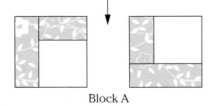

Sew this seam. Be certain to keep all pairs
oriented this way until all are sewn.

Block A

Fig. 47

fullest width, cut between the pieces with cutter,
and make the unit as square as possible (Fig. 46).

Everyone
As soon as you have 40 done, you have completed
Block A. Make Block B exactly the same way but use
Color #2 in place of Color #1.

When 80 blocks are completed, lay them out in the
predetermined arrangement.

Cutter and Presser
Divide Block A blocks into two piles, orienting them
as in Fig. 47, and hand them to the Stitcher.

Stitcher
Flipping a block from the right-hand pile over a
block from the left-hand pile, sew the A blocks into
twos, feeding them through without lifting the presser foot, keeping the edges even.

Presser
Snip apart the string of twos and press all seams
away from the Color #3 square.

Cutter
Add the pressed twos to the layout, turning them to
fill in the pattern. (In Fig. 48, all the Block A blocks
were sewn as 1A – 2A pairs, but turning them makes
them into 3A – 4A pairs.)

(Note: If you are using the other layout, your fabrics
may be oriented differently, but the numbers will be
the same.)

Cutter and Presser
Divide the Block B blocks into two piles, orienting
them correctly (See 5B-6B in Fig. 48). Hand the pairs
of Block B blocks to the Stitcher.

Pieces of Eight

Stitcher

Flipping a block from the right-hand pile over a block from the left-hand pile, sew the B blocks into twos, feeding them through without lifting the presser foot, keeping the edges even.

Presser

Snip apart the string of twos and press all seams away from the center square.

Cutter

Add the pressed twos to the layout, turning the twos to fill in the pattern. (In Fig. 48, all the Block B blocks were sewn as 5B/6B pairs, but turning them makes them into 7B/8B pairs.)

Presser and Cutter

Flip the 1A – 2A twos over the 3A – 4A twos and put a pin in the seam (Fig. 49). Hand them to the Stitcher. Do the same with the Block B blocks, flipping the 5B – 6B twos over the 7B – 8B twos.

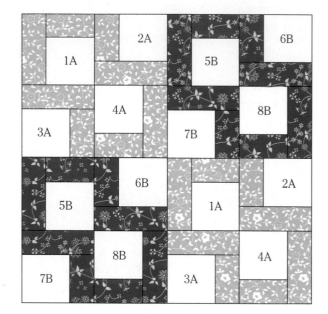

Fig. 48

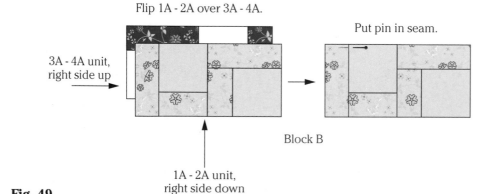

Flip 1A - 2A over 3A - 4A.

Put pin in seam.

3A - 4A unit, right side up

Block B

1A - 2A unit, right side down

Fig. 49

Stitcher

Sew the pinned seams and from here on, keep the seams and edges matched. Hand the fours back to the Presser.

Presser

Press seams toward 1A – 2A and toward 7B – 8B. At this point you have a fours that looks like a figure 8.

Presser and Cutter

Layout the fours again. Now take fours in the first column and flip 5B – 6B – 7B – 8B over 1A – 2A – 3A – 4A, pin seams to be sewn, and hand them to the Stitcher

Working down the first column, flip the next 1A – 2A – 3A – 4A over 5B – 6B – 7B – 8B, pin the seam to be sewn and pass these pieces to the stitcher. Continue for the length of the quilt. Repeat with the next column. (Press the seams toward 1A – 2A – 3A – 4A).

Stitcher

Sew the seams by feeding the blocks through the machine without lifting the presser foot. When all eight blocks are together across the quilt, sew the remaining seams.

Presser

Press all the seams in the same direction. Now add the border (see Chapter 3). Don't forget to prepare the backing of your quilt.

Helpful Tip

Every quilt should have a label proclaiming who made it and for what occasion it was made. Why not make your own personal label from fabric that matches your quilt? To keep the fabric taut while writing, use freezer paper. Draw evenly spaced parallel lines as a guide on the non-shiny side of freezer paper with a black marking pen. Press the shiny side of the freezer paper to the wrong side of the fabric. Then, using a permanent pen, write on the fabric along your guide lines. You may need to use a light table to make the lines easier to see. When you are finished writing, remove the freezer paper, turn under raw edges, and hand sew the label to your quilt. This is a simple trick but a neat one — the paper adds stability to the fabric, and the lines on the paper help make your label especially neat.

English Log Cabin

English Log Cabin

This quilt provides space for a marvelous quilting design or a large floral fabric.

Menu

Melon Cup, p. 116

Taco Salad, p. 119

Pam's Corn Bread, p. 121

Luscious Dessert Cake, p. 123

Quilt Sizes

Finished size double – 81" x 102" includes 3¾" border

Finished size queen – 90" x 111" includes 8¼" border

Size before border – 73½" x 94½"

Number of blocks – 63 (7 blocks x 9 blocks)

Number of blocks A (pieced block) – 31 for each layout

Number of blocks B (light): Layout 1 – 20

Layout 2 – 12

Layout 3 – none

Layout 4 – 32

Number of Blocks C (dark) Layout 1 – 12

Layout 2 – 20

Layout 3 – 32

Layout 4 – none

Finished block size – 10½"

Finished border width double – 3¾"

Finished border width queen – 8¼"

Note: For layouts 1, 2, and 3 on p. 74, Colors #1, 3, and 5 are dark colors; Colors #2, 4, and 6 are light. For layout 4, Colors #1, 3, and 5 are light and Colors #2, 4, and 6 are dark.

Block Samples

Block A

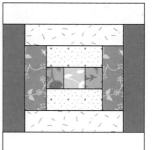

Block B

Block C

Color Key

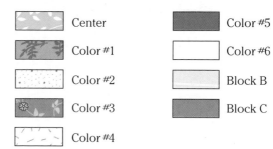

Center

Color #1

Color #2

Color #3

Color #4

Color #5

Color #6

Block B

Block C

English Log Cabin

Layout Samples

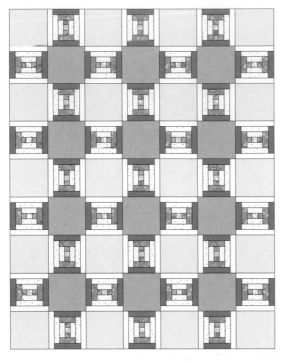

Layout 1 with more light blocks

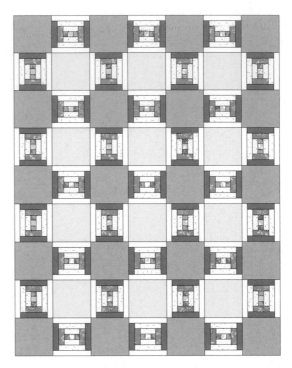

Layout 2 with more dark blocks

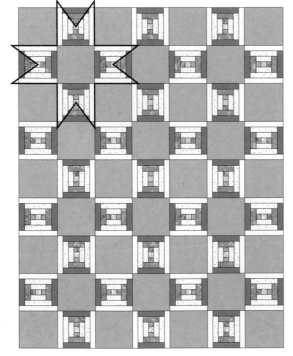

Layout 3 with no light blocks

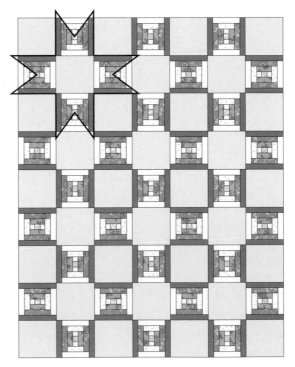

Layout 4 with no dark blocks

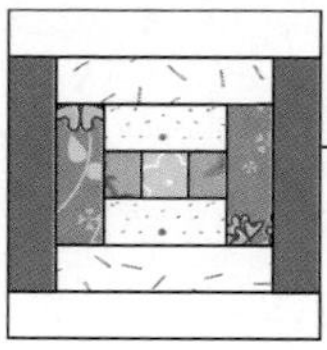

Fabric Requirements (44/45" fabric)

Pieced Blocks		Unpieced Blocks
Center – ¼ yard	Color #4 – 1 yard	If you use 12 – 1½ yards
Color #1 – ¼ yard	Color #5 – 1 yard	If you use 20 – 2½ yards
Color #2 – ⅝ yard	Color #6 – 1⅓ yards	If you use 32 – 3⅞ yards
Color #3 – ⅝ yard		

	Double		Queen	
One border	3¾"	1½ yards	8¼"	2¾ yards
Binding		¾ yard		1 yard
Backing		6 yards		8 yards

Quilt top owner

Determine the layout you wish to use before buying your fabric and make sure your coworkers know which layout you plan to use so the piecing process can move along.

Putting the team to work

Stitcher

Adjust the machine to a shorter than average stitch length because you will be cutting across seams. Try a seam on scrap fabric to get a ¼" seam, and fill two or three bobbins with a neutral thread.

Cutter

Fold your fabric and even the raw edges. Then, cut two 2" strips of Center fabric and three 2" strips of Color #1 across the width of fabric.

Presser

Give one strip of the Center fabric and two strips of Color #1 to the Stitcher, then cut the other Center strip and the other Color #1 strip in half.

Stitcher

Sew a Color #1 strip onto each side of the Center strip. Do the same with the three half strips. These strip sets will look like Fig. 50, p. 76.

Cutter

From Colors #2 – #6, cut the following number of 2" strips:

Color #	Cut Size	# of Strips
2	2"	8
3	2"	7
4	2"	13
5	2"	13
6	2"	16

Start with Color #2 and stop to cut the strip sets into pieces as described below but stay ahead of the Stitcher.

Presser

It is best to press all the seams away from the center. If one fabric is too dark and shows on the right side more than desired, you can break this rule.

Normally, on the wrong side, lightly press the seams away from the center. Turning to the right side, press the strip set to the fullest possible width, keeping the set as straight as possible.

English Log Cabin

Cutter

Line your ruler up with the seams as in Fig. 51 and cut this strip set into 2" pieces. Count these — you need 31 pieces. Give these to the Stitcher with the Color #2 strips. (After you have cut a few pieces, realign the ruler to make sure the cuts are still straight.)

Keep your hands flying while you chat!

Stitcher

Lay strip Color #2 right side up on the machine. Lay a pieced section right side down on top of it starting just below the selvage. Feed the pieced sections through without stopping, butting each one exactly together (Fig. 52). As soon as you have one strip filled, pass it to the Presser. Continue until all 31 pieces are sewn onto the strips of Color #2.

Presser

Lay the strip on the table with Color #2 down, pieced sections up. Press the seam flat and straight and cut between the pieced sections with scissors (Fig. 53). If the Stitcher has left a gap between the pieces, you must cut the same space from the bottom strip. If she has overlapped the pieces, you are all in trouble. No need to re-press at this time. When the Stitcher has finished sewing all the pieced sections to the strips of Color #2, give her the pieces you have cut with another strip of Color #2.

Stitcher

Lay another strip of Color #2 on the machine and add the pieced sections you just cut. Start below the selvage (Fig. 54, p. 78). Continue sewing all 31 pieces onto the strips.

Presser

Lay the pieced sections on the ironing table as before, pieced side up. Press the seam flat and cut

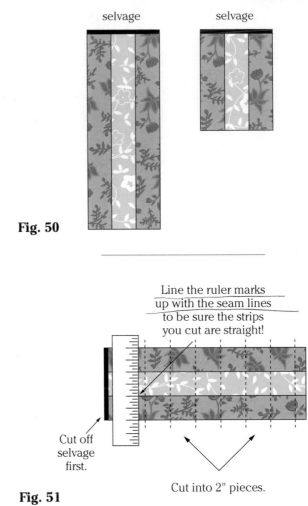

Fig. 50

Line the ruler marks up with the seam lines to be sure the strips you cut are straight!

Cut off selvage first.

Cut into 2" pieces.

Fig. 51

between pieces. Once again, if there are gaps between the pieced sections, you must cut the same space from the bottom strip. Press both seams away from the center, keeping the block as square as possible.

At this point, you need to make sure your block is square. Measure it carefully with a square template or ruler. If you are not cutting, pressing, or sewing properly, your block will begin to get disfigured.

When the Stitcher has finished sewing the pieces onto the strips of Color #2, give her the pieces you have just cut with a Color #3 strip.

Start below selvage.

Pieced section of Center fabric and Color #1 fabric, right side down

Carefully place pieced sections right next to each other, abutting but not overlapping.

Strip of Color #2 right side up

Fig. 52

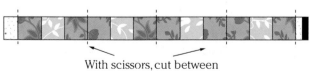

With scissors, cut between pieced sections.

Fig. 53

Stitcher

Lay the Color #3 strip on the machine. Lay the pieced sections on the strip and sew as before (Fig. 55, p. 78).

Presser

Lay the strip on the table, Color # 3 right side down with the pieced sections up. Press the seam flat and straight and cut between the pieced sections. No need to press this time; you only need to press seams when both pieces of the same color are on. Give the strip to the Stitcher with another strip of Color #3.

> **Helpful Tip**
>
> When you have a quilt with a large unpieced block like the one in the English Log Cabin, it lends itself to a lovely design of hand quilting, embroidery, stenciling, or even one of the preprinted cheater blocks.

Stitcher

Lay another strip of Color #3 on the machine and add the pieced sections that were just cut. Remember to start below the selvage.

Presser

Lay this section on the ironing table as before, pieced side up. Press the seam flat and cut between the pieces. Once again, if there are gaps between the pieced sections, you must cut the same space from the bottom strip.

Press both seams away from the center, keeping the block as square as possible. Give these back to the Stitcher with a Color #4 strip to start the process over again.

After Color #4 is on, measure your block carefully again to be sure it is square.

English Log Cabin

Everyone

Continue adding the strips to make the block. Notice that as you repeat the procedure you are always putting two strips of the same color on the blocks you are building. They are always opposite each other. All odd numbers are together and all even numbers are together.

Cutter

As soon as a few blocks are completed with all six colors sewn on, measure two or three. Take an average of this measurement and cut the number of light and/or dark squares for the chosen pattern in this size.

You may cut these from the length of the fabric or the width, whichever you prefer. To speed up the process, take two strips, lay them together and cut into squares and continue with pairs of strips until you get the number of squares needed.

Everyone

Lay the blocks out in the chosen design (Fig. 56). Notice as you lay out that the pieced block alternates position.

Presser and Cutter

Start with the first two columns, flipping #2 over #1, #4 over #3, etc. Pin these together as in Fig. 57 so you know which edge to sew.

Stitcher

Sew the first two columns into twos, feeding pieces through without lifting the presser foot.

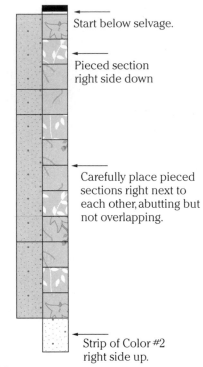

Start below selvage.

Pieced section right side down

Carefully place pieced sections right next to each other, abutting but not overlapping.

Strip of Color #2 right side up.

Fig. 54

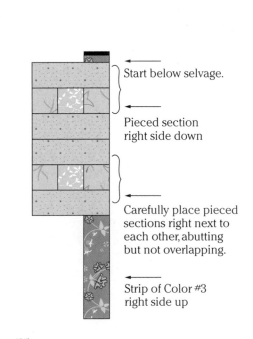

Start below selvage.

Pieced section right side down

Carefully place pieced sections right next to each other, abutting but not overlapping.

Strip of Color #3 right side up

Fig. 55

		Columns				
1	2	3	4	5	6	7
1	2	19	20	37	38	55
3	4	21	22	39	40	56
5	6	23	24	41	42	57
7	8	25	26	43	44	58
9	10	27	28	45	46	59
11	12	29	30	47	48	60
13	14	31	32	49	50	61
15	16	33	34	51	52	62
17	18	35	36	53	54	63

Fig. 56

Everyone

Return the twos to the layout and repeat the process with columns 3 and 4, and 5 and 6. Next flip column 3 – 4 over 1 – 2 to make fours. Continue until you have nine rows down and six blocks across. Add the last block to each row.

Presser

Press all seams in row one to the left, row two to the right, row three to the left, alternating the direction of the pressed seam in each successive row.

Stitcher

Sew all nine rows together, matching the block corners as closely as possible.

Presser

Press the seams carefully.

Oh! Don't you love it? Now it is time for the border. Refer to Chapter 3. Remember to prepare the backing to be ready for finishing.

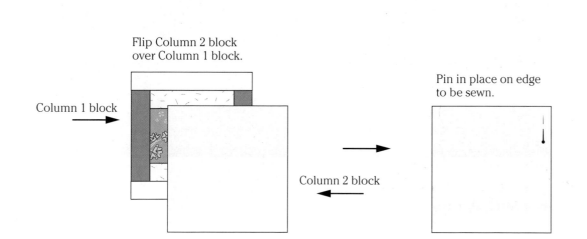

Flip Column 2 block over Column 1 block.

Column 1 block

Column 2 block

Pin in place on edge to be sewn.

Fig. 57

Double Irish Chain

Double Irish Chain

This is an old favorite. A little more work, but worth it.

Menu

Apricot Refresher, p. 116

Crunchy Crab Salad, p. 117

Cheese Turnovers, p. 120

Betty's Easy X-cellent
 Berry Pie, p. 122

Quilt Sizes

Finished size double – 81" x 101" includes 5½"
 border

Finished size queen – 90" x 110" includes 10"
 border

Size before border – 70" x 90"

Number of blocks – 63 (7 blocks x 9 blocks)
 Block A – 32, Block B – 31

Finished block size – 10"

Finished border width double – 5½"

Finished border width queen – one 10" or one
 4½" and one 5½"

Block Sample

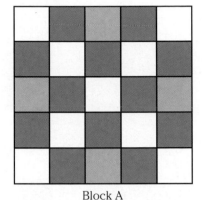

Block A

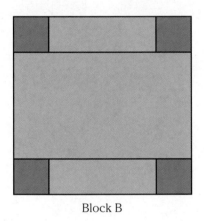

Block B

*The Double Irish Chain was traditionally done in
green and white. Now the sky is the limit. A large floral looks stunning as Color #3, especially if you are
tying your quilt. If you are quilting, Block B invites an
elaborate quilting design.*

Color Key

Color #1   Color #2   Color #3

Double Irish Chain

Layout Sample

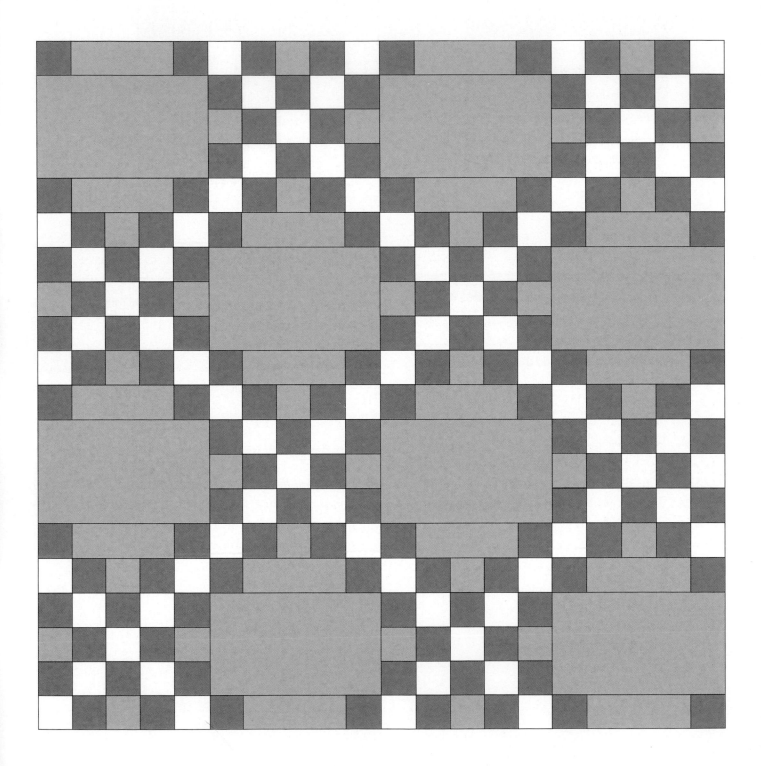

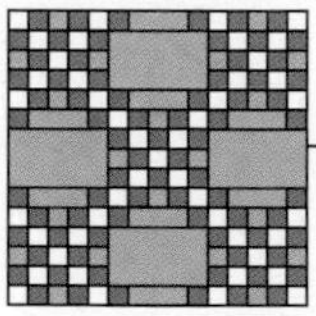

Fabric Requirements (44/45" fabric)

| Color #1: 1¾ yards |
| Color #2: 2¾ yards |
| Color #3: 3¾ yards |

	Double		Queen	
One Border	5½"	1¾ yards	10"	3 yards
Two Borders	—	—	or { 4½"	1⅝ yards
	—	—	5½"	2 yards
Binding	¾ yard		⅞ yard	
Backing	5⅞ yards		8 yards	

Putting the team to work

Assembling Block A

Stitcher

Adjust the machine to a shorter than average stitch length because you will be cutting across seams. Try a seam on scrap fabric to get a ¼" seam and fill two or three bobbins with neutral thread.

Cutter

Fold your fabric and even the raw edges. Then cut one 2½" strip of Color #1 and one 2½" strip of Color #2, cutting across the width of the fabric. Give to Stitcher. Cut a 2½" strip of Color #3 and another of #2 and #1 and hand to the Stitcher. As she gets started on these strips continue cutting all the strips, as directed in chart below. Cut pieces of each color, rather than cutting all the same color at the same time so the Stitcher will always have strips of each color ready.

Strips for Block A (cut across width of fabric)

Color #	Cut Size	# of Strips
1	2½"	18
2	2½"	24
3	2½"	8

Presser

Give strips from the Cutter to the Stitcher in the order needed to make the strip sets in Fig. 58. You will need four of Strip set 1, four of Strip set 2, and two of Strip set 3.

Stitcher

Sew four of Strip set 1, four of Strip set 2 and two of Strip set 3.

Presser

Pressing all seams toward the darkest fabric, press each strip set to the fullest width, keeping the set as straight as possible.

Cutter (or Presser)

As each strip set is pressed, cut off one selvage edge, aligning ruler lines with seams (Fig. 59, p. 84). Cut 2½" across the fabric to make 2½" strips from each of the sets. Each set should yield 16 or 17 pieced strips. You need 64 pieces from each of Sets 1 and 2, and 32 from Set 3. (After you have cut a few pieces, realign the ruler to make sure it has not slipped.) Label each pile and hand Sets 1 and 2 to Stitcher.

Double Irish Chain

Stitcher

Now sew the pieced strips together to make the block, matching the seams, and sewing one strip from Strip Set 2 to one from Strip Set 1 without lifting the presser foot until all the strips of Strip Sets 1 and 2 are sewn into twos.

Cutter

Count out 32 strips of Set 3 and give them to the Stitcher.

Stitcher

Add Set 3 strips to the Set 2 side of half of the twos you've just sewn without lifting the presser foot between strips. Make sure Set 2 ends up in the middle (Fig. 60, p. 85).

When you have used all the Set 3 strips, sew the remaining twos to the threes, making sure each Set 2 piece is between a Set 3 piece and a Set 1 piece. The Set 3 piece in each block should end up in the middle (Fig. 61, p. 85).

Hooray! Block A is now ready to be pressed — all seams in the same direction. But before pressing them, take time to get Block B ready for the Stitcher.

Assembling Block B
Cutter

Cut two 2½" strips of Color #2 and one 6½" strip of Color #3 to get the Stitcher started. Then continue cutting these strips.

Color #	Cut Size	# of Strips
2	2½"	8
3	6½"	4
3	10½"	6

(These are approximate measurements; adjust the size of Block B to match that of Block A, if necessary.)

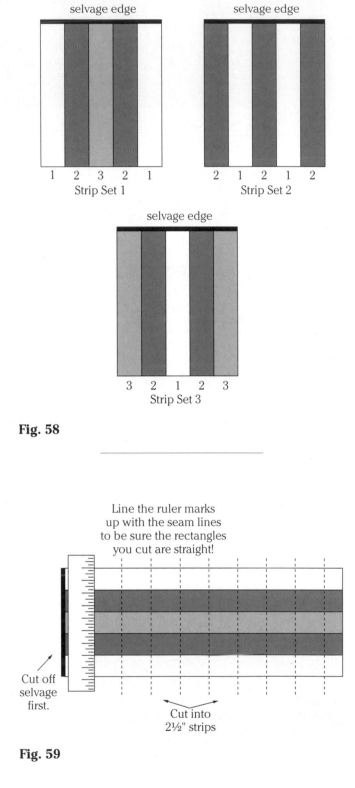

Fig. 58

Fig. 59

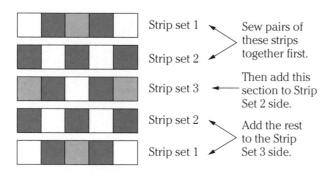

Strip set 1

Strip set 2

Strip set 3

Fig. 60

Strip set 1 ⟶ Sew pairs of these strips together first.

Strip set 2 ⟶

Strip set 3 ⟵ Then add this section to Strip Set 2 side.

Strip set 2 ⟶ Add the rest to the Strip Set 3 side.

Strip set 1 ⟶

Fig. 61

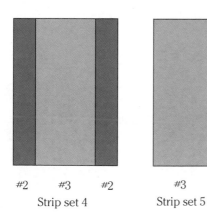

#2   #3   #2   #3

Strip set 4   Strip set 5

Fig. 62

Presser

Give these to the Stitcher in the order needed to make the sets in Fig. 62. Strip 5 needs no sewing; the 10½" strips of Color #3 are complete as cut.

> **Helpful Tip**
> When pressing strip sets, it is a good idea to lightly press the seam first on the wrong side; then press on the right side, gently pulling the strip set to the fullest width as you press.

Stitcher

Sew four of Strip set 4.

Presser

Press seams toward darker fabric.

Cutter

Cut across Strip set 4, making 2½" strips as shown in Fig. 59; each set should yield 16 – 17 pieces. You need 62.

> **Helpful Tip**
> If you haven't made your seams exactly ¼" when assembling Block A, the block won't be exactly 10½". Adjust the center strip of Block B to make this block closer to the size of Block A. Measure the interior three rows of Block A on the right side of the fabric. Measure your actual seam size and double that measurement. Add this amount to the center measurement to account for seaming and cut your four strips of Color #3 this width.

Cutter

Cut Strip 5 (your approximate 10½" strips) into approximately 6½" pieces. You need 31 pieces.

Stitcher

Following Fig. 63, sew the pieces from Strip 5 to the 31 pieces of Strip set 4, and the rest of the pieces

> **Helpful Tip**
> Carefully folded fabric can make all the difference when cutting your pieces. A crooked fold may result in wasted fabric or elbow-shaped pieces. Take the time to make sure the fabric is smooth and evenly folded.

Double Irish Chain

from Strip set 4 to the opposite side of the Strip 5 pieces. Block B is now ready to be pressed.

Presser

Press each Block A with all seams going in the same direction. Press Block B seams away from the center strip.

Joining your blocks together

Presser and Cutter

Before laying out the blocks, set aside 5 Block A's and 4 Block B's. From the remaining blocks pass them in pairs to the Stitcher, alternating the position of A and B blocks as shown in Fig. 64. Keep the seams in the B blocks going the same direction.

Stitcher

Flip Column 2 blocks over Column 1 blocks and sew the right-hand seam, matching the two seams at the arrow points in Fig. 64.

Sew the pairs without lifting the presser foot. Keep seams in the B block all going in the same direction. Pass them on to your helpers as you sew the nine pairs together.

Presser and Cutter

Snip the threads and lay out nine pairs down and three across as in Fig. 65. Give the pairs to the Stitcher so she can make the pairs into fours, and then pass her the final pairs to make them into sixes.

Stitcher

Sew the pairs into fours without lifting the presser foot, then add the third column of pairs to make sixes in the same manner.

Presser and Cutter

Snip the threads between the nine sixes. Using the

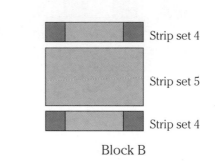

Strip set 4

Strip set 5

Strip set 4

Block B

Fig. 63

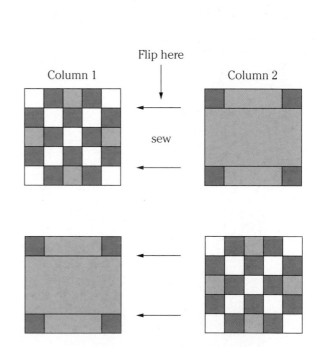

Fig. 64

A	B		A	B		A	B
B	A		B	A		B	A
A	B		A	B		A	B
B	A		B	A		B	A
A	B		A	B		A	B
B	A		B	A		B	A
A	B		A	B		A	B
B	A		B	A		B	A
A	B		A	B		A	B

Fig. 65

nine blocks you set aside, add one to each of the sixes following your alternating pattern.

Presser

It is easiest on your Stitcher if you press the seams left on the first row and right on the second row, etc. However, if this quilt is to be hand quilted, the quilter might like all seams going in the same direction.

Stitcher

Sew all nine rows together across the quilt. Match the block corners and seams as closely as possible.

Presser

Press seams carefully.

Now your quilt is ready for the border. Refer to Chapter 3 for directions. Prepare the backing of your quilt for finishing.

Rail Fence

Rail Fence

This is an easy one! No nerves needed here!

Menu

Cathy's Apricot Salad, p. 116

Cheesy Broccoli Soup, p. 117

Ma Barnes' Oatmeal Bread, p. 120

Carrot Cake, p. 123

Block Sample

Quilt Sizes

Finished size double – 81" x 97" includes 4½" border

Finished size queen – 90" x 106" includes 9" border

Size before border – 72" x 88"

Number of blocks – 99 (9 blocks x 11 blocks)

Finished block size – 8"

Finished border width, double – 4½"

Finished border width, queen – one 9" or one 3½" and one 5½"

Color Key

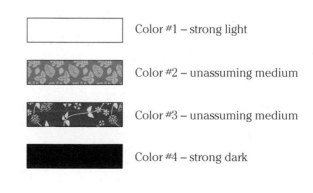

Color #1 – strong light

Color #2 – unassuming medium

Color #3 – unassuming medium

Color #4 – strong dark

Rail Fence

Layout Sample

A	B	A	B	A	B	A	B	A	Row 1
C	D	C	D	C	D	C	D	C	Row 2
A	B	A	B	A	B	A	B	A	Row 3
C	D	C	D	C	D	C	D	C	Row 4
A	B	A	B	A	B	A	B	A	Row 5
C	D	C	D	C	D	C	D	C	Row 6
A	B	A	B	A	B	A	B	A	Row 7
C	D	C	D	C	D	C	D	C	Row 8
A	B	A	B	A	B	A	B	A	Row 9
C	D	C	D	C	D	C	D	C	Row 10
A	B	A	B	A	B	A	B	A	Row 11

Fig. 70

over the next A square and feed it under the presser foot right after the previous squares. Continue to stitch your squares into 24 twos this way, feeding one after the other. Hooray! No seams to match, just keep the edges even.

Everyone

Repeat this procedure with piles C and D, flipping D squares over C squares to make 20 twos, feeding them through as before.

You now have 24 twos of A/B and 20 twos of C/D blocks. Put these together into 11 rows of eight blocks each as shown in Fig. 70. Take your A/B twos and sew them together to make fours. Then sew these fours together to make 11 eights.

Then take your C/D twos and sew them together to make fours. Take these C/D fours and sew them together to make eights. Be sure to keep your A/B blocks and your C/D blocks separate!

Cutter and Presser

Once this is done, bring out the 11 blocks you put aside. Hand them one at a time to the Stitcher.

Stitcher

Using the 11 unused blocks, sew an A to the last B in the odd rows and a C to the last D in the even rows. You should now have 11 strips of 9 blocks each.

Presser

Press the seams in odd numbered rows in one direction and seams in the even rows in the other direction.

Stitcher

Sew all rows together, butting seams.

Presser

Press all seams carefully in the same direction.

Congratulations! All that's left for today is the border (see Chapter 3). Prepare the backing in your spare time so it will be ready to tie or baste for quilting.

Kissing Nine-Patch

Kissing Nine-Patch

There are a lot of Nine-Patch quilts out there, but this is the first one we've ever caught kissing.

Menu

Melon Cup, p. 116

Chicken Salad, p. 117

Easy Cheesy Garlic Rolls, p. 120

Betty Patton Sheet Cake, p. 122

Quilt Sizes

Finished size double – 81" x 91½" includes 3¾" border

Finished size queen – 90" x 100½" includes 8¼" border

Size before border – 73½" x 84"

Number of blocks – 56 (7 blocks x 8 blocks)

Finished block size – 10½" inches

Finished border width double – 3¾"

Finished border width queen – 8¼"

Block Sample

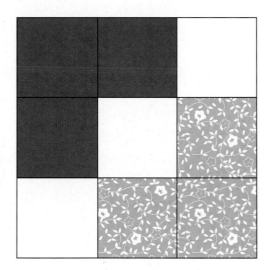

Color Key

 Color #1

 Color #2

Color #3

Kissing Nine-Patch

Layout Samples

In this layout the contrasts are pronounced, and the kiss really stands out.

Kissing Nine-Patch

This is the Diagonal Nine-Patch layout. Notice the large square is not present here, and the effect is different. The small blocks look like stairs.

Diagonal Nine-Patch

Fabric Requirements (44/45" fabric)

Color #1: 2¼ yards
Color #2: 2¼ yards
Color #3: 2¼ yards

	Double		Queen	
Border	3¾"	1½ yards	8¼"	2⅝ yards
Binding		¾ yard		⅞ yard
Backing		5½ yards		7 yards

Quilt top owner

Determine which layout you want to follow and be sure your colleagues know your choice to avoid chaos when it is time to put your quilt together. Lucky you! You have chosen an easy one — only one block design.

Putting the team to work

Stitcher

Adjust the machine to a shorter than average stitch length because you will be cutting across seams. Try a seam on scrap fabric to get a ¼" seam and fill two or three bobbins with neutral thread.

Cutter

Fold your fabric and even the raw edges then cut two strips of Color #1 and one strip of Color #3, each 4" wide, across the width of the fabric. Keep ahead of Stitcher and continue cutting until you have cut the total number of strips in chart below.

Color #	Cut Size	# of Strips
1	4"	18
2	4"	18
3	4"	18

Presser

Lay out the strips according to the diagram. As the Stitcher is ready, give her the strips needed to make six strip sets of each layout in Fig. 71.

Stitcher

Sew six strip sets of each of the combinations in Fig. 71.

Presser

As strip sets are sewn, take them to the pressing table and press each seam flat. On the wrong side, lightly press seams in all Strip sets 1 and 3 toward the center strip and all Strips sets 2 away from the center strip. (Exception: If Color #3 is the darker color, press Strip set 1 away from the center, Strip set

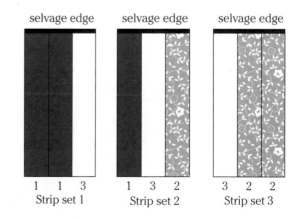

Fig. 71

2 toward the center, and Strip set 3 away from the center). Turn the sets to the right side and press to the fullest possible width. Continue until all are pressed.

Cutter

As sets are pressed, line up the ruler along the seams as in Fig. 72. Cut off one selvage edge and continue cutting into 4" pieces across the width of the fabric. (After you have cut a few pieces, realign the ruler to keep your pieces straight and true.)

Presser

Lay the pieces out as in the block sample. Flip the piece from Strip set 2 over the piece from Strip set 1 and pin as in Fig. 73 with the point of the pin marking the spot where the Stitcher should start sewing. Continue pinning the pieces together (Strip set 2 over Strip set 1) and give all of them to the Stitcher. (These pieces are pinned to ensure that the correct seams are sewn. However, if the Stitcher does not want to use pins, occasionally check to be sure the correct seam is being sewn.)

Stitcher

Feed the pieces through the machine without lifting the presser foot.

Cutter

Snip the pieces apart. Give the sewn pieces to the Presser.

Presser

Add a piece from Strip set 3 to each sewn pair, pinning the piece to the Strip set 2 side of the pair, making sure it is aligned as in Fig. 74.

Stitcher

Sew all the Strip set 3 pinned pieces without lifting the presser foot.

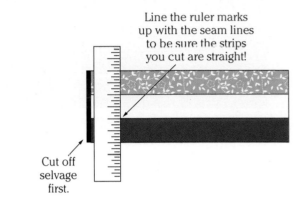

Line the ruler marks up with the seam lines to be sure the strips you cut are straight!

Cut off selvage first.

Fig. 72

Flip here

Strip set 1 Strip set 2

= 2 flipped over 1, right sides together

Fig. 73

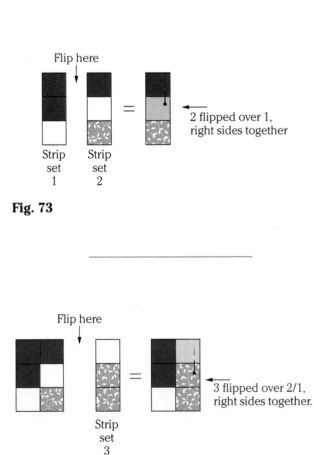

Flip here

Strip set 3

= 3 flipped over 2/1, right sides together.

Fig. 74

Kissing Nine-Patch

Columns

1	2	3	4	5	6	7
1	2	17	18	33	34	49
3	4	19	20	35	36	50
5	6	21	22	37	38	51
7	8	23	24	39	40	52
9	10	25	26	41	42	53
11	12	27	28	43	44	54
13	14	29	30	45	46	55
15	16	31	32	47	48	56

Fig. 75

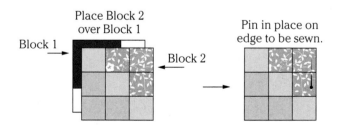

Fig. 76

Presser

Press all the seams in one direction.

Presser and Cutter

Lay the blocks out in the predetermined layout (Fig. 75), beginning with the first two columns. Flipping #2 over #1, #4 over #3, and so on, flip the second column of blocks over the first column. Pin as in Fig. 76 so you know which edge to sew. Make all the twos you can from all the blocks by continuing with the third and fourth columns and then the fifth and sixth. (Keep in mind if you have seven columns you will have one column remaining at right that is not used now.) Depending on the layout you choose, each pair of columns may be identical to the other column pairs. If that is the case, all your twos will be the same. However, your layout may involve different column pairs. If so, you will have to be careful not to mix up your twos. Double check your layout.

Stitcher

Sew all the blocks together into twos at the pinned seam, feeding them through without lifting the presser foot. Be careful to match seams and edges.

Presser and Cutter

Lay out all twos again in the proper order. You now have three twos across each row plus one extra square in each row. Take the 17 – 18 pair and flip over the 1 – 2 pair, pin on the seam to be sewn and hand to Stitcher to sew into fours. Continue down the first two columns (flip 19 – 20 over 3 – 4, 21 – 22 over 5 – 6) until the first two columns are made into fours.

Kissing Nine-Patch

Stitcher

Sew all the twos together into fours at the pinned seam, matching seams.

Presser and Cutter

Using the third column of twos, take the 33 – 34 twos and flip it over the 1 – 2 – 17 – 18 fours and pin on right side. Give this to the Stitcher to sew into a six. Continue down your rows (flip 35 – 36 over 3 – 4 – 19 – 20) and pass them to the Stitcher until you have eight sixes with only the last column of single blocks left to attach.

Stitcher

Sew all the blocks into sixes at the pinned seam as they are handed to you.

Presser and Cutter

Pin the seventh block in each row to the sixes that you have created and pass to the Stitcher.

Stitcher

Sew the extra block on each row at the pinned seams.

Presser

Press all seams in the top row toward the left, and all seams in the next row toward the right, continue, alternating rows.

Stitcher

Sew all eight rows together, matching the block corners and seams as closely as possible.

Presser

Press seams carefully all in the same direction.

Next step — add the border (see Chapter 3). Prepare the backing to be ready to finish your quilt.

Mock Jacob's Ladder

Even simple designs can be gorgeous. This quilt was a grand prize winner!

Mock Jacob's Ladder

Menu

Lentil Soup, p. 118

Cheesy Snack Bread, p. 120

Betty's Date Pudding, p. 122

Quilt Sizes

Finished size double – 81" x 100½" includes 6½" border

Finished size queen – 90" x 109½" includes 10½" border

Size before border – 68¼" x 87¾"

Number of blocks – 63 (7 blocks x 9 blocks)

Block A – 32; Block B – 31

Finished block size – 9¾"

Finished border width double – 6½"

Finished border width queen – one 10½" or one 4" and one 6½"

Block Sample

Block A

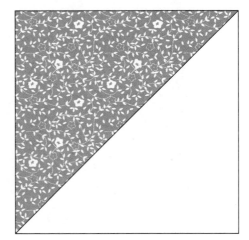

Block B

Color Key

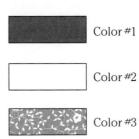

Color #1

Color #2

Color #3

Layout Samples

Mock Jacob's Ladder

Stars of a Different Color

Elongated Star

The same squares were used with all three of these layouts, the squares have simply been rearranged. Which one catches your fancy?

Mock Jacob's Ladder

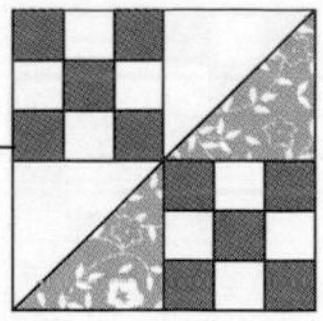

Fabric Requirements (44/45" fabric)

	Color #1: 2 yards Color #2: 3½ yards Color #3: 2 yards			
	Double		**Queen**	
One Border	6½"	2 yards	10½"	3¼ yards
Two Borders	—	—	or { 4"	1¼ yards
	—	—	6½"	2⅛ yards
Binding	¾ yard		⅞ yard	
Backing	5⅞ yards		8 yards	

Quilt top owner

Make the tough decisions first. Determine which layout you would like to use and let your coworkers know your choice.

Putting the team to work

Assembling Block A

Stitcher

Adjust the machine to a shorter than average stitch length because you will be cutting across seams. Try a seam on scrap fabric to get a ¼" seam, and fill two or three bobbins with neutral thread.

Cutter

Fold your fabric and even up the raw edges. Cut two 3¾" strips of Color #1 and one 3¾" strip of Color #2 across the width of fabric. Give these to the Stitcher. Continue cutting all strips listed in chart below — be sure to have the colors ready before the Stitcher needs them.

Color #	Cut Size	# of Strips
1	3¾"	15
2	3¾"	12

Presser

As the strips are ready, give them to the Stitcher in the order needed to make strip sets in Fig. 77.

Stitcher

Sew six of Strip set 1 and three of Strip set 2.

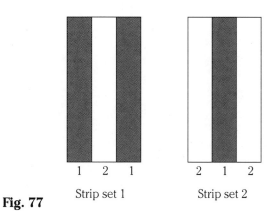

Strip set 1   Strip set 2

Fig. 77

Presser

On the wrong side, lightly press the seams toward the darkest fabric. Turn to the right side and press each strip set to the fullest width, keeping strip as straight as possible.

Cutter

As each strip set is pressed, align ruler lines with a seam as in Fig. 78. Cut off one selvage edge and con-

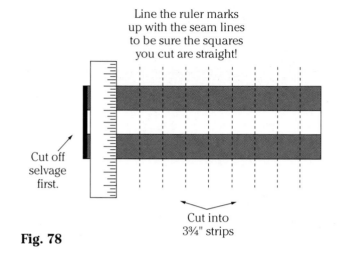

Line the ruler marks up with the seam lines to be sure the squares you cut are straight!

Cut off selvage first.

Cut into 3¾" strips

Fig. 78

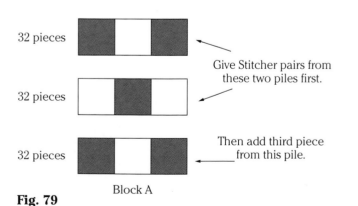

32 pieces

32 pieces

Give Stitcher pairs from these two piles first.

32 pieces

Then add third piece from this pile.

Block A

Fig. 79

tinue cutting across the set to make 3¾" strips. (After you have cut a few pieces, realign the ruler so you do not end up with crooked strips.)

You should get 11 3¾" pieces from each strip set. You need 64 from Strip set 1 and 32 from Strip set 2.

Presser

Separate the blocks into three piles of 32 — 32 pieces from Strip set 1; 32 pieces from Strip set 2; and 32 more pieces from Strip set 1. Lay out in Block A arrangement as in Fig. 79. Give the stitcher the top two piles.

Stitcher

Taking a piece from each pile, sew 32 pairs together, butting seams and keeping edges even.

Presser

Give the Stitcher the 32 pieces of Set 1 from your third pile.

Stitcher

Sew the remaining 32 pieces from Set 1 onto the pairs you just finished, making sure the piece from Set 2 is in the middle.

Presser

Press all seams one way. Measure a few of the pieces — they should be 10¼". If a happy average isn't 10¼", you will need to adjust the size you cut the strips of Block B. Block B strips should be cut about ⅜" larger than the average size of the Block A strips.

Assembling Block B

Cutter

Cut 4 strips approximately 10⅝" across the width of Color #2, and 4 strips approximately 10⅝" across the

Mock Jacob's Ladder

width of Color #3, adjusting for the size of Block A as noted above.

Lay strips of Colors #2 and #3 right sides together and cut into (approximately) 10⅝" squares. Hold carefully so neither fabric slips as you cut. Keep these square pairs together and cut them diagonally once from one corner to another (Fig. 80). Each square yields two triangular pairs. (You need 16 squares of each color, a total of 32 triangles). Extra yardage is included in case you cannot cut four across the width of the fabric.

Presser
Keep these triangle pairs together — don't let them shift even a little bit — and give each pair to the Stitcher.

Stitcher
Sew the diagonal edge of the pair, feeding pairs through without lifting the presser foot. Be careful not to stretch the bias edge.

Presser
Press seams toward the darkest fabric.

Presser and Cutter
Lay the blocks out in the predetermined layout (Fig. 81). Work with the first two columns first, flip #2 over #1, #4 over #3, etc. Put a pin in the side to be seamed with the point of the pin marking the place where the Stitcher should start sewing (Fig. 82).

Stitcher
Sew the first 2 columns into twos.

Everyone
Return these to the layout and repeat with columns 3 and 4, then 5 and 6. Next flip column 3 – 4 over 1 – 2 to make fours. Continue until you have nine rows

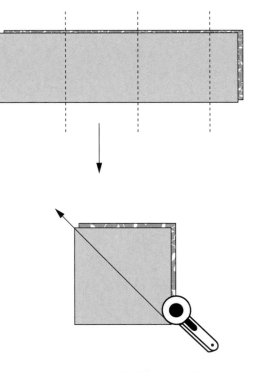

Put strip of Color #2 over strip of Color #3, right sides together.

Wrong side up

Right side up

Cut into 10⅝" squares, keeping strips together.

Cut squares diagonally in one cut from one corner to another. Keep triangle pairs together.

Fig. 80

Mock Jacob's Ladder

Columns

1	2	3	4	5	6	7
1	2	19	20	37	38	55
3	4	21	22	39	40	56
5	6	23	24	41	42	57
7	8	25	26	43	44	58
9	10	27	28	45	46	59
11	12	29	30	47	48	60
13	14	31	32	49	50	61
15	16	33	34	51	52	62
17	18	35	36	53	54	63

Fig. 81

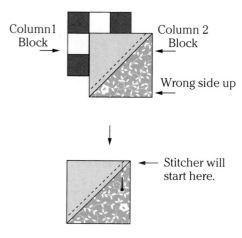

Fig. 82

down and six blocks across. Add the last block to each row.

Presser
Press all seams either toward the Nine-Patch block or the triangle block, whichever best suits your fabric.

Helpful Tip
To minimize the confusion when moving blocks between the layout table and the sewing machine, put a pin in the side to be seamed with the point of the pin marking where the Stitcher should start the seam. If you do this consistently, the Stitcher can locate where to begin, saving everyone time.

Stitcher
Sew all 9 rows together, matching the block corners.

Presser
Press seams carefully, all in the same direction.

Now add the border (Chapter 3). Don't forget to prepare the backing of your quilt.

Rings of Color

Inspired by "Sticks and Stones" by Marti Michell.

American Patchwork and Quilting, August 1993

Menu

Marinated Carrots, p. 116

Fruit and Cheese Salad, p. 117

Cloud Biscuits, p. 120

May's Strawberry Meringue
 Shortcake, p. 124

Block Sample

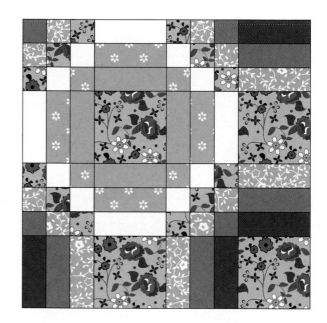

Quilt Sizes

Finished size double – 81" x 104¾" includes 10¼" on 3 sides and 6¾" on top

Finished size queen – 90" x 109" includes 14½" on 3 sides and 6¾" on top

Size before border – 60¾" x 87¾"

Number of blocks – 6 plus extra mini blocks on top and left side

Finished block size – 27"

Finished mini block size – 6¾"

Finished border width double – 6¾" and 3½" (as above) 3 sides total: 10¼

Finished border width queen – 6¾" and 7¾" (as above) 3 sides total: 14½

Color Key

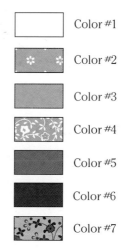

☐ Color #1

▦ Color #2

▨ Color #3

▨ Color #4

▨ Color #5

■ Color #6

▨ Color #7

Rings of Color

Mini Blocks

Nine-Patch
Need 28
strips

Rail A
Need 24
strips

Rail B
Need 34
strips

Plain Block
Need 35
strips

Layout Sample

Check out the chapter on choosing your fabric for several examples of this quilt (pages 12-14).

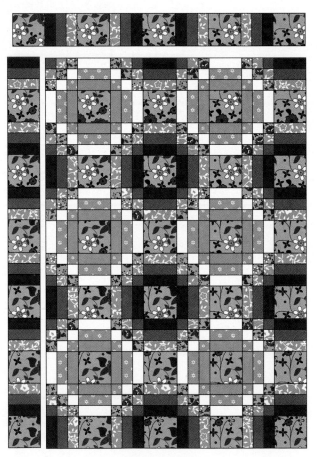

This layout shows the effect if lighter colors are used for
Colors 1, 2, and 3.

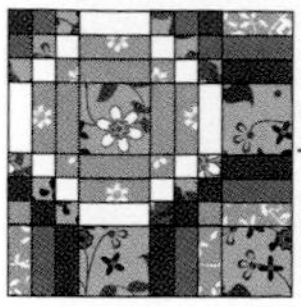

Fabric Requirements (44/45" fabric)

Color #1: 1 yard	Color #5: 1 yard
Color #2: ¾ yard	Color #6: ¾ yard
Color #3: ½ yard	Color #7: 2⅓ yards
Color #4: 1¼ yards	

		Double			Queen	
One border	3 sides	10¼"	2⅓ yards	3 sides	14½"	3¼ yards
	Top	6¾"	¾ yard	Top	6¾"	¾ yard
Binding		⅞ yard			1 yard	
Backing		6⅛ yards			8 yards	

Note: If you prefer multiple borders instead of the wide ones, get a little extra total fabric.

Putting the team to work

This beautiful quilt is a challenge because the block is made out of several mini blocks and is not symmetrical so putting it together can be confusing. The extra pieced border you add to the top and one side balances your quilt. Relax, take a deep breath, take it step by step, and you will be fine.

Stitcher

Adjust the machine to a shorter than average stitch length because you will be cutting across seams. Try a seam on scrap fabric to get a ¼" seam, and fill two or three bobbins with a neutral thread.

Cutter

Cut strips 2¾" wide across the width of the fabric. Cut one each of Colors #7, #4, and #5 to get the Stitcher started on the Nine-Patch mini blocks. Try to keep her supplied with the strips she needs next, following the chart below. Keep cutting until you have cut the total of 2¾" wide strips listed in the chart.

Presser

Give one strip each of Colors #7, #4, and #5 to the Stitcher. Help arrange them in order, following Fig. 83, p. 112. Keep the Stitcher supplied as needed. It may be easiest to put together both sets of the Strip Set 1 configuration, both of Strip set 2, both of Strip Set 3, and then move on to Strip sets 4 and 5. If you choose to do it that way, have your Cutter cut the strips of Colors #7, 4, 5, 1, and 2 that you'll need first for Strip sets 1, 2, and 3.

Color #	# of Strips, 2¾" wide	# of Strips, 7¼" wide
1	8	Do not cut these until you have measured the Nine-Patch mini blocks.
2	6	
3	4	
4	10	
5	8	
6	6	
7	6	6

Stitcher

Sew all strip sets as shown in Fig. 83, p. 112, beginning with Strip set 1. Place the strip of Color #7 right side up on the machine and place the strip of Color #4 on top of it, right side down, and sew the seam. Open the sewn strips and lay a strip of Color #5 on top of the pieced strip right side down directly on

Rings of Color

top of Color #4. Sew the seam and pass the set to the Presser who will give you the strips for the next strip set.

Presser

On the wrong side, lightly press the seams of Strip set 1 toward Color #7 (unless it shows too much on the right side, in which case, press the seam toward the darker fabric). Turn right side up and press the set to the fullest possible width, keeping it as straight as possible.

Press the seams of Strip set 2 toward Color #4 and Strip Set 3 toward Color #2.

Press the seams of Rail Strip sets toward the darkest fabric.

Cutter

Align the ruler marks with the seams and cut Sets 1, 2, and 3, into 2¾" pieces, cutting off the selvage first. See Fig. 84. You should have 28 of each. (After you have cut a few pieces, realign the ruler to guard against error.) Lay them out into the Nine-Patch mini blocks.

Stitcher

Take the pieces for the Nine-Patch mini block layout and sew all pieces from Strip set 2 onto Strip set 1, feeding the pairs through the machine without lifting the presser foot. Then add pieces from Strip set 3 (Fig. 85). Be sure the pieces from Strip set 2 end up in the middle and are all properly oriented.

Presser

Press the seams in one direction on the Nine-Patch mini blocks.

Cutter

The Rail Strip sets should be the same size as the

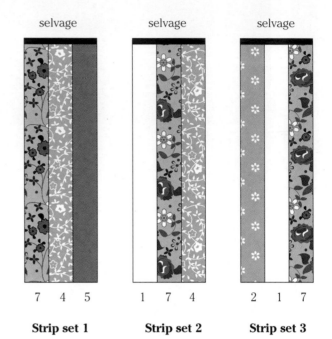

selvage   selvage   selvage

7   4   5   1   7   4   2   1   7

Strip set 1   Strip set 2   Strip set 3

Strip sets 1, 2, and 3 are used
to make the Nine-Patch mini block.
Sew 2 strip sets each.

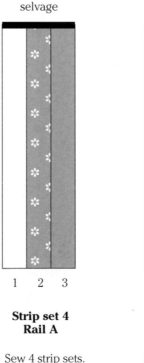

selvage   selvage

1   2   3   4   5   6

Strip set 4   Strip set 5
Rail A   Rail B

Sew 4 strip sets.   Sew 6 strip sets.

Fig. 83

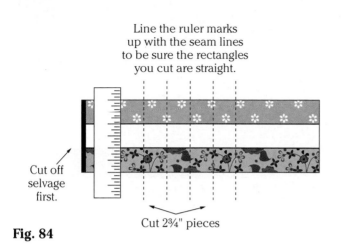

Line the ruler marks
up with the seam lines
to be sure the rectangles
you cut are straight.

Cut off
selvage
first.

Cut 2¾" pieces

Fig. 84

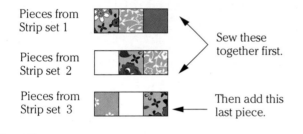

Pieces from
Strip set 1

Pieces from
Strip set 2

Pieces from
Strip set 3

Sew these
together first.

Then add this
last piece.

Fig. 85

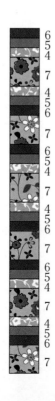

Fig. 86

Nine-Patch mini blocks (approximately 7¼"). Measure the width of the Rail sets in a few places and take an average measurement (hopefully very close to 7¼"). Cut the sets into this size squares. You need 24 from the Rail A sets and 34 from Rail B sets.

Cutter

Now that you know the width of the Nine-Patch mini blocks, you can cut Color #7 into strips the same size as the Nine-Patch mini blocks, approximately 7¼". Cut into squares of which you need 35.

Everyone

Regroup! Everyone who is free should lay out the mini blocks into the six large blocks following the block sample on page 109. Give these to the Stitcher in the most organized manner you can devise. You may want to simply treat each large block as a unit and put together the four mini blocks in the top row, then return them to the layout. Put together the next row of four mini blocks and return them to the layout; then do the next row of four and the next. Then sew the four, four-block rows together and start with the next block. It is a good idea to press each row as soon as it is sewn, first row to the left, second row to the right, etc.

When the six big blocks are completed, lay them out as in the layout sample, making sure you have two blocks across and three down.

Cutter and Presser

Hand the large blocks to the Stitcher in pairs, pinning the seam to be sewn with the tip of the pin marking where the Stitcher should start sewing.

Stitcher

Sew together each pair of large blocks (you will end up with three pairs), then sew the three pairs together until you have a 2 x 3 block unit. If you make sure there's always a Nine-Patch in the upper left hand corner you'll keep it straight.

Presser

Press the seams in the first pair to the left, the seams in the second to the right, etc.

Cutter and Presser

Lay out the left side column of mini blocks as shown in Fig. 86, p. 113, alternating plain blocks (Color #7) and Rail B blocks, orienting them correctly. Hand these to the Stitcher in the proper order.

Stitcher

Sew the left side column together as pictured (Fig. 86, p. 113).

Presser

Press these seams. It is best to press seams to butt with the others but if that is too confusing, just press them all one way.

Stitcher

Add this to the left side of the quilt, being careful to match seams as closely as possible.

Cutter and Presser

Lay out the top row of blocks as in Fig. 87, alternating plain blocks (Color #7) and Rail B blocks, orienting them correctly. Hand these to the Stitcher in the proper order.

Stitcher

Sew together the top row of mini blocks as in Fig. 87 (hand to the Presser to press) and add to the top of

> **Helpful Tip**
> Pressing seams in alternating directions whenever possible will make a less bulky seam and also make it easier to match seams when butting them.

7 6 5 4 7 4 5 6 7 6 5 4 7 4 5 6 7

Fig. 87

> **Helpful Tip**
> To keep blocks or pieces in order between the layout table and the sewing machine, place a small, removable sticker in the upper left-hand corner of each, far enough from the edge not to catch in the seam. Remove the sticker before ironing.

the quilt, being careful to match seams as closely as possible.

Presser

Press all seams carefully.

Take a well-deserved few minutes to stretch and have a rejuvenating lunch. You can do the border while you are digesting. You have four Nine-Patch mini blocks remaining. You may use them in corners of your first border if you wish; if you have chosen to use multiple borders just make sure you cut your first border the width of the blocks. See Chapter 3 for border instructions. Remember to put the backing together when you have a few minutes free so you will be ready to baste or tie your masterpiece.

Chapter 6

Recipes

All recipes serve 6 (unless otherwise noted), can be doubled if necessary, and made ahead, except for last minute touches or warming.

Side Dishes & Appetizers

❦

Main Dishes

❦

Breads

❦

Desserts

❦

Snacks, Cookies & Goodies

Recipes

Side Dishes & Appetizers

Apricot Refresher

Hardly a recipe!

Give each person a small scoop of lemon sherbet. Pour on a little apricot nectar, about ¼ –⅓ c. Eat with a spoon for a refreshing appetizer.

Cathy's Fruited Apricot Salad

Tart — a gelatin surprise

Heat one 12-oz. can (1½ c.) apricot nectar to boiling. Add one 3-oz. pkg. lemon flavored gelatin; stir until it's dissolved. Add ½ c. water and 1 Tbsp. lemon juice. Chill till partially set.

Fold in: one 11 oz. can drained mandarin orange sections
        ½ c. seedless grapes, halved
        ¼ c. chopped apple

Turn into a 4-cup mold and chill until firm. Unmold. Serve with mayonnaise.

Crisp Noodle Cabbage Salad

A different twist on cabbage

Chop: 1 head cabbage
        1 onion
        2 carrots

Dressing: 3 Tbsp. sugar
        2 Tbsp. vinegar
        ½ tsp. salt
        ½ tsp. pepper
        ½ c. vegetable oil
        Beef or chicken flavor packet from ramen noodles.

Add dressing to cabbage. Refrigerate.

Brown: 3 Tbsp. sunflower seeds
        ½ c. slivered almonds.

Stir in pan over low heat with 1 tsp. butter.

Just before serving, top salad with nuts, seeds, and 1 package ramen noodles, crumbled but not cooked. Serves 12.

Glazed Fruit Cup

Dresses up any fruit

Mix any combination of the following (fresh or canned) to make 6 cups: bananas, pineapple, apples, grapes, peaches, kiwi, strawberries, or melons. In saucepan, mix ½ c. orange juice concentrate with ½ c. water. Thicken with 1 Tbsp. cornstarch. Stir constantly on medium heat. Cool. Fold into fruit.

Marinated Carrots

Called "copper pennies"

Cook until tender crisp: 2 lbs. carrots sliced into ¼" rounds
Combine:

    1 can tomato soup, undiluted
    ¾ c. vinegar
    ½ c. cooking oil
    1 tsp. Worcestershire sauce
    1 tsp. dry or prepared mustard
    ½ tsp. salt
    ⅔ c. sugar

Pour sauce over:
    Carrots
    2 thinly sliced onions
    2 thinly sliced green peppers

Marinate in refrigerator 24 hours or more. Serves 12.

Melon Cup

Perfect summertime dish

Use any melons you like — cantaloupe, honeydew, watermelon, etc. Remove the seeds and scoop the flesh out in balls or cut into cubes for easy eating. Chill before serving. Add a small scoop of orange sherbet to each serving.

Nutty Fruit Salad

Good anytime

Mix together:
    2 oranges, remove seeds and membranes from orange sections and cut in half
    2 c. seedless grapes
    2 bananas, sliced
    2 apples, diced
    1 tsp. lemon juice

Add just before serving:
    ½ c. salted almonds or mixed nuts
    ½ c. cubed cheese (cheddar, Swiss, or whatever you fancy)

Dressing: ½ c. French dressing
    2 Tbsp. grated cheese.

Top each serving with a splash of dressing.

Simple All Season Salad

Crunchy and tangy

Break up enough lettuce and/or spinach for 6 people. Wash, dry and chill. Drain an 11 oz. can mandarin oranges. Slice ½ large sweet onion. Break into rings. Melt 1 tsp. butter and brown ½ c. sliced almonds in skillet over low heat until lightly browned.

Dressing: ¼ c. vegetable oil
    1 Tbsp. sugar
    ¼ c. seasoned rice vinegar

½ tsp. salt

¼ tsp. pepper

Put all dressing ingredients together in a blender and blend for a few seconds. Just before serving, toss everything together.

Sweet Greek Salad

Nice winter salad when tomatoes are terrible

Cut or break enough lettuce and/or spinach for 6 people into salad size pieces.

Add: ½ c. sweet onion slices, separated into rings and cut in quarters

11 oz. can mandarin oranges, drained

1 medium can pitted black ripe olives

1 c. feta cheese

Toss and serve with a Greek dressing that has a little sugar added to it. (Sugar is optional but adds to the taste.)

Waldorf Salad

Always a favorite

3 c. diced apples

1½ c. sliced celery

1½ c. seedless grapes

½ c. walnut halves

1 c. miniature marshmallows (optional)

Combine:

½ c. salad dressing

½ c. heavy cream, whipped

2 tsp. sugar

Fold into fruit mixture. Chill.

Main Dishes

Cheesy Broccoli Soup

Rich and delicious — a crockpot triumph

Sauté ½ lb. mushrooms lightly. Cook 2 – 10 oz. packages broccoli, slightly. Drain and chop. Put both in crockpot and add:

2 cans cream of mushroom soup

½ pound cheddar cheese, grated

1 can (rinse out soup can) white wine

1 can (rinse out other soup can) milk

Dash of tarragon

Cook on low for a couple of hours. Make sure cheese melts.

Chicken Salad

Devised in May's kitchen

Combine the night before so everything is well chilled.

Drain: 1 can (11 oz.) mandarin oranges

1 can (20 oz.) pineapple tidbits

3 c. cooked chicken, chopped

2 c. seedless grapes

¼ c. chopped sweet onion

¼ c. chopped green peppers

½ c. chopped celery

One hour before serving mix with: 1 cup salad dressing to which 2 Tbsp. seasoned rice vinegar and 1 Tbsp. sugar have been added. Just before serving, top salad with 1 c. salted cashews or toasted sliced almonds.

Crunchy Crab Salad

A good healthy lunch

2 pkg. (10 oz.) frozen baby peas, thawed, uncooked

1 c. chopped celery

2 c. chopped cauliflower (uncooked)

½ c. chopped sweet onion

1 lb. shredded crab meat (or other seafood if preferred)

In bowl, mix 1 cup sour cream and enough of a package of dry ranch dressing mix to make it taste good to you (or use a dressing of your choice). Toss with veggies and crab.

Fruit and Cheese Salad

So pretty

Mix : 1 pkg. (3 oz.) cream cheese

1 Tbsp. honey

Stir in 1 c. sour cream and chill.

Combine 2 c. shredded mild cheddar cheese

1 small head shredded lettuce

In a large glass bowl layer:

lettuce mixture

2 c. strawberry slices

2 c. peach slices

2 c. seedless grapes

cream cheese mixture

For the best results, make 2 layers each.

Ham and Biscuit Dinner

Hearty and delicious

Combine in large casserole:

2½ c. cubed, cooked ham

15 oz. can whole kernel corn, drained

1½ c. diced cooked potatoes

Recipes

¼ c. minced parsley (or celery leaves)

2 Tbsp. minced onion

1 c. grated carrots

½ tsp. salt

¼ tsp. dry mustard

¼ tsp. paprika

⅛ tsp. black pepper

Melt 4 Tbsp. butter or margarine in saucepan. Add 2½ Tbsp. flour, stir until smooth. Gradually add 2¼ c. milk. Cook, stirring constantly, until thickened.

Pour over ingredients in casserole. Top with biscuits, made from one of the recipes in bread section or biscuit mix. Bake at 400° 35 – 40 minutes until heated through and biscuits are done.

Leftover Turkey/Broccoli Bake

Great for those Thanksgiving leftovers

Grease or spray sides of 9x13 baking dish with cooking spray. Spread ¾ c. turkey gravy in bottom. Add a layer of cut up turkey (about 4 c.). Add another ¾ c. gravy and another layer turkey (about 4 c.). Top this with 2 – 10 oz. packages frozen broccoli, partially cooked and drained. Dribble on ½ lb. cheese spread melted, (melts easy in microwave) or more if you like. Top with a layer of flavored croutons. Cover with foil and bake at 350° for about 30 minutes. Uncover and bake 10 minutes more to be sure croutons are crisp. Serves 12.

Lentil Soup

Hearty — a meal in itself

Brown ½ lb. hot Italian sausage, crumbled

      ½ lb. low fat ground beef

Drain off fat.

Stir in and brown slightly:

      1 large onion, chopped

      1 small green pepper, chopped

Add: 2 carrots, chopped

      1 minced garlic clove

      1 quart canned tomatoes

      4 cups water

      6 chicken bouillon cubes

      2 cups dry lentil beans

      ¼ tsp. black pepper

      ¼ tsp. curry powder

      1 bay leaf (remove before eating)

      1½ tsp. dry mustard or 1 Tbsp. prepared mustard

      Salt to taste

Cook until beans are tender, about 1 hour. Add 4 c. water or vegetable juice. Serves 12.

Potato Dried Beef Bake

Great to warm you on cold days

Peel and cut 6 medium potatoes into eighths and cook until fork tender. While cooking, cut 6 – 8 oz. of sliced dried beef into small pieces.

Melt 4 Tbsp. butter in frying pan and sauté dried beef until butter starts to brown. Stir in 4 Tbsp. flour and gradually add 2 c. milk or half and half, stirring constantly until it thickens. Salt to taste and add a dash of pepper.

Drain potatoes and put into glass baking dish or casserole. Pour on gravy. Top with a handful of crushed potato chips and bake uncovered in 350° oven until heated through, 35 – 45 minutes, and potatoes are done.

Seedy Baked Chicken

A special treat

Sauté: 1 c. chopped celery

      ½ c. onion

      ½ c. mushrooms in 2 Tbsp. melted butter or margarine

Remove from heat.

Mix: 1½ c. crumpled round butter crackers

      4 Tbsp. butter or margarine

      3 Tbsp. poppy seeds

Spread ½ of cracker mixture in bottom of 2½ qt. casserole.

To sauté, add:

      2 lbs. (6 – 8 cups) chopped chicken, cooked and deboned (boneless breast works well)

      1 can cream of chicken soup, undiluted

      8 oz. sour cream

      2 c. frozen peas

      ½ tsp. salt

      sprinkle of black pepper

Spoon into casserole on top of crackers. Spread remaining cracker crumbs on top and bake at 350° for 45 – 60 minutes or until bubbly.

Sweet and Sour Beef and Cabbage Dinner

May also be reheated to serve later

In large skillet (electric is handy), cook until browned:

      1½ lbs. ground beef

      ½ c. chopped onion

      ½ c. sliced celery

      ½ c. green pepper

Drain off fat, sprinkle with:

      2 Tbsp. rolled oats

      2 Tbsp. parsley

      ¾ tsp. salt

      ¼ tsp. garlic powder

Core 1 medium cabbage and cut in wedges. Place on meat. In a bowl, make a sauce of :

> 1 can (15 oz.) tomato sauce
> ¼ c. cider vinegar
> ½ tsp. salt
> ¼ tsp. black pepper
> ¼ c. brown sugar

Mix well. Pour over cabbage and meat. Cover and simmer 20 – 30 minutes until cabbage is tender. Serve immediately.

Taco Salad
Help yourself

Everyone will put together their own salad. In separate bowls, set out:

> 1 head shredded lettuce
> 2 or 3 pkgs. (8 oz.) any ready shredded cheese
> 4 – 6 medium tomatoes, cut into small pieces
> 1 medium bag any flavor taco chips, crushed slightly
> 1 or 2 jars salsa sauce
> 1 bottle blue cheese dressing or 8 oz. sour cream
> 1 or 2 cans refried beans, heated in microwave

> 1 large sweet onion, sliced

Just before serving, in electric frying pan, brown 1½ lbs. lowfat ground beef, adding salt and pepper to taste.

Zesty Spaghetti Salad
Extra good when all the veggies are garden fresh

> ¾ lb. broken spaghetti — cooked and cooled
> ½ c. sweet onion, chopped
> 2 tomatoes, chopped
> 1 cucumber, chopped
> ½ green pepper, chopped
> ½ c. black olives
> ¼ c. green olives
> 6 radishes, chopped
> ½ c. celery, chopped
> ¾ c. grated parmesan cheese
> A few fresh or a small can of mushrooms

Mix together all ingredients and refrigerate. One or two hours before serving, stir in 8 oz. zesty Italian dressing and add enough salad dressing to make as moist as desired, return to refrigerator.

Breads

Betty's Lemon Bread
Almost cake

Mix:
> 1 c. sugar
> ⅓ c. margarine (melted)
> 2 eggs

Sift:
> 1½ c. flour
> 1 tsp. baking powder
> 1 tsp. salt

Add flour mixture to sugar mixture alternately with:
> 2 Tbsp. lemon juice
> ½ c. milk

Add: ½ c. nuts, chopped fine

Pour into one regular size greased bread pan. Bake at 350° for 45 – 50 minutes or until done.

While baking make glaze of:
> ¼ c. lemon juice
> ½ c. sugar

Bring to boil and pour on bread as it comes out of the oven while still hot.

Brown Bread
The old-fashioned way or when your oven is on the blink

Mix together:
> 1½ c. raisins
> 2 c. whole wheat flour

> ½ c. white flour
> ½ c. corn meal
> 1 tsp. salt
> 1 tsp. baking soda
> 2 c. milk
> ¾ c. molasses

Pour into 2 greased and floured 1 pound coffee cans. Cover each filled can tightly with aluminum foil and set in a tall kettle of boiling water that comes half way up the coffee cans. Cover kettle and boil until bread is done, or when a toothpick inserted into the center comes out clean. (You may also bake in two bread pans in a 350° oven for 45 – 60 min.)

Buttermilk Biscuits
An old standard

Sift:
> 2 c. flour
> 3 tsp. baking powder
> ½ tsp. salt

Cut in: ⅓ c. shortening until mixture resembles coarse crumbs. Make a well in the middle. Add ¾ c. buttermilk. Stir just until moistened. Turn onto lightly floured surface. (Dough will be soft). Knead gently with the heel of your hand 10 – 12 strokes. Roll or pat to ½" thick. Cut with floured biscuit cutter straight down, no twisting, or cut in squares. Bake 12 – 15 minutes at 450° on ungreased strip set. Makes 12 – 16 biscuits.

Recipes

Cheese Turnovers

So easy with frozen bread dough

To make filling mix:

> ½ cup cottage cheese
>
> 4 oz. shredded cheddar cheese
>
> 1 small egg, beaten
>
> ½ c. chopped parsley
>
> ¼ c. chopped onion

Thaw 1 loaf frozen uncooked bread dough and cut into 12 pieces. Separate and place on greased cookie sheet. As soon as dough starts to rise, roll each piece in a circle, 5 inches in diameter. Place a spoonful of filling over half of the circle, keeping edges clean. Fold in half and seal by pressing bottom edge over top edge. With scissors, cut slits in top to allow steam to escape. Place on greased baking sheet, allow to rise slightly, and bake at 400° for 10 – 15 minutes, until lightly browned.

Cheesy Snack Bread

Delicious wedges full of cheese

Soften: 1 pkg. yeast in ¼ c. warm water.

Scald: ¼ c. milk and let cool to lukewarm. (Milk is scalded when a film shows on the top as you blow gently on the surface.)

Meanwhile, in mixing bowl sift:

> 1½ c. flour
>
> 1 Tbsp. sugar
>
> ½ tsp. salt
>
> ¼ tsp. black pepper

Cut in ⅓ c. butter or margarine.

Add 1 beaten egg, softened yeast, and milk.

Beat well and stir in:

> ½ c. grated parmesan cheese
>
> 2 Tbsp. chopped parsley
>
> 1 Tbsp. sesame or poppy seeds

Turn into greased 8" x 1½" round cake pan. Dot with a little more butter. Cover with damp cloth and let rise in a warm place until double, about 40 minutes. Bake at 375° oven 20 – 25 minutes. Cut in pie-shaped wedges and serve warm.

Cloud Biscuits

So light and fluffy

Sift together:

> 2 c. all-purpose flour
>
> 4 tsp. baking powder
>
> ½ tsp. salt

Cut in ½ c. margarine until mixture resembles coarse crumbs.

Combine and add all at once:

> 1 beaten egg
>
> ⅔ c. milk

Stir until batter follows fork around bowl. Turn out on lightly floured surface. Knead gently about 20 strokes. Roll to ¾" thickness. Cut. Place on ungreased baking sheet — close for soft biscuits, ¾" apart for crusty ones. Bake at 450° for 10 – 14 minutes. May be chilled 1 – 3 hours before baking. Makes 12 biscuits.

Easy Cheesy Garlic Rolls

Fantastic served warm

Thaw 1 loaf frozen bread dough. As soon as dough is thawed, cut into 12 pieces and roll into balls. Place in a greased 9" round cake pan. Put in a warm place until it just starts to rise.

While dough is rising, stir together:

> ⅓ c. grated cheese (any kind you like)
>
> 1 tsp. garlic powder
>
> ½ stick butter, melted

With scissors, snip an X in the top of each roll. Pour cheese mixture over rolls in pan. Cover and let rise until doubled. Bake at 375° for 10 –15 minutes.

Easy Sticky Buns

So delicious and so easy

2 dozen Parker house rolls, frozen and unbaked, cut in half and placed into greased 9x13 pan.

Sprinkle with topping:

> 1 pkg. (3 oz.) regular vanilla pudding mix
>
> ½ c. brown sugar
>
> ½ c. raisins (optional)
>
> ½ c. nuts

Sprinkle with cinnamon and pour 1 stick melted margarine over all. Let set overnight (or 8 hours) in refrigerator. If dough has risen in the fridge, bake right away for 30 minutes at 350°. If it hasn't risen, let it sit out in a warm spot until it rises a bit and then bake. Remove from oven. Turn upside down on plate. Remove pan immediately.

Ma Barnes' Oatmeal Bread

Boy, could she make bread

Soften 1 pkg. dry yeast in ⅔ c. warm water.

Mix together:

> 2 c. boiling water
>
> ½ c. sugar
>
> 1 tsp. salt
>
> 1½ Tbsp. shortening
>
> 1 c. oatmeal (either quick or regular rolled oats)

Cool to lukewarm and add the yeast mixture and 2½ c. flour. Stir until stiff (at this point, you could add about 2 cups of raisins). Gradually stir in another 2½ c. flour.

Knead the bread, adding flour as necessary. Hopefully you'll get away with 6½ c. total of flour used. Knead 5 – 10 minutes, until satiny. Let rise until doubled. Divide into two loaves and make smooth. Roll loaf in more oats or sesame or poppy seeds. Let rise again. Bake at 350° for about 40 minutes.

Maple Nut Muffins

Great made with syrup straight from the tree

Mix together :

> 2 c. flour
> ¼ c. firmly packed brown sugar
> 1½ tsp. baking powder
> ¼ tsp. salt

In small bowl, beat 1 egg.

Stir in: ½ c. maple syrup
> ⅓ c. butter or margarine, melted
> ½ c. milk
> 1 tsp. vanilla

Add to flour mixture and stir just until moistened. Batter will be lumpy. Stir in 1 c. chopped pecans. Spoon into greased muffin pan, filling each ⅔ full.

Topping: 1 Tbsp. sugar
> ⅛ tsp. cinnamon

Spread topping over each muffin.

Bake 15 – 20 minutes at 400°. Makes 12 muffins.

Pam's Corn Bread

Perfectly sweetened

Mix: 1¼ c. flour
> ¾ c. yellow cornmeal
> ½ c. sugar
> 2 tsp. baking powder
> ½ tsp. salt

Stir in: 1 c. whole milk
> ¼ c. vegetable oil
> 1 egg, beaten

Mix until moistened and pour into greased 8" or 9" baking pan. Bake at 350° 25 – 30 minutes until golden brown. Serve warm.

Refrigerator Bran Muffins

Easy to dip into for a quick treat

Pour 2 c. boiling water over 2 c. bran cereal. Set aside. Cool.

Sift together:

> 5 c. sifted flour
> 5 tsp. baking soda
> 2 tsp. salt

Cream: 2 c. sugar
> 1 c. shortening

Add: 4 eggs, well beaten

Mix: 1 qt. buttermilk, and 4 c. bran buds cereal

Add: Bran cereal as prepared above

Add: Flour mixture

Stir until moistened. Store in sealed container in refrigerator up to 5 weeks. Makes 5 doz. Bake as needed in greased muffin tins at 400° for 10 – 15 minutes.

Sour Dough Biscuits

A delicious biscuit

Sift together:

> 1½ c. sifted flour
> 2 tsp. baking powder
> ½ tsp. baking soda
> ½ tsp. salt

Cut in: ¼ c. butter or margarine

Add: 1 cup sour dough starter mix

Knead dough on floured board until satiny. Roll ½" thick. Cut with 2½" biscuit cutter or in squares. Place on ungreased baking pan and brush with melted butter. Let rise one hour in warm place. Bake at 425° for 20 minutes. Serve warm. Makes 12 biscuits.

Sour Dough Starter

Good for biscuits, pancakes, bread, doughnuts, etc.

Boil some peeled potatoes (about 4), in plenty of water to cover. Do what you will with the spuds but save the water. Mix 2 cups of lukewarm potato water with 2 cups flour, 1 Tbsp. sugar, and 1 tsp. salt.

Put in a crock and stand in a warm spot, loosely covered 3 or 4 days or until it is working merrily and has attained a peculiar and delightful odor. "She'll let you know when she's up," the old timers say. You'll see what they mean. You may add 1 tsp. dry yeast, but if you have time, let it take its natural course. When ripe, store in refrigerator. Replace what you use with equal amounts of flour and enough water to give original consistency. Let work again in warm place and refrigerate.

Desserts

Betty's Date Pudding

Lush, but so easy

Sift 1 tsp. soda over ½ lb. dates cut in small pieces. Pour 1 c. boiling water over the dates. Let cool.

Cream: 1 c. sugar
         1 Tbsp. butter
Add: 1 egg
Sift together and add:
         1½ c. flour
         1 tsp. baking powder
         ½ tsp. salt
         1 tsp. vanilla
         ½ c. chopped nuts

Add the date mixture. Stir and pour into greased 9" x 13" pan. Bake at 375° for 30 – 35 minutes or until done.

While baking,

Mix: another ½ lb. cut up dates
         ½ c. nuts
         1 c. sugar
         ⅔ c. hot water

Cook on top of stove until it melts together and comes to a boil. Pour over pudding as soon as it comes from oven. This is fine made the day before and reheated. Serve with whipped cream or ice cream. Serves 12.

Betty's Easy X-cellent Berry Pie

Ah! strawberry season

1 baked pie shell (9 in.) Buy or make your own from one of the recipes in this section. Soften 8 oz. cream cheese with 2 Tbsp. sugar. (If you don't use light cream cheese, you may have to add a little milk to make it spreadable.) Spread in bottom of baked pie shell. Wedge full of fresh ripe strawberries. Glaze with freezer or regular strawberry jam that has been thinned with a touch or water. You don't need much — depending on how sweet your berries are, use about ¼ to ½ c. Top with whipped cream or ice cream.

Betty's Never Fail Pie Crust

Makes 5 crusts

Sift together: 4 c. flour
                 2 tsp. salt
                 1 Tbsp. sugar
Cut in: 1¾ c. vegetable shortening
Mix together:
                 ½ c. cold water
                 1 extra large egg

                 1 Tbsp. vinegar

Pour liquid into flour mixture and form into 5 equal flattened balls. Wrap each in waxed paper or plastic wrap. If using immediately, refrigerate ½ hour to make dough easy to handle.

The balls can be stored in a refrigerator a day or two and in the freezer longer, if desired. Let soften before rolling into pie shell. For a baked shell, prick with fork and bake at 425° for 8 – 10 minutes or until browned slightly. Don't prick the crust if your recipe calls for an unbaked shell... the filling will leak through.

Betty Patton Sheet Cake

How can something so good be so easy?

Stir in bowl: 2 c. flour
                2 c. sugar
Put in sauce pan and bring to boil:
                1 stick margarine
                ½ c. vegetable shortening
                3 Tbsp. cocoa
                1 c. water
Pour over flour mixture and stir.

Add 1 tsp. baking soda to ½ c. buttermilk and add to chocolate mixture. Add 2 slightly beaten eggs and 1 tsp. vanilla. Pour into greased 11" x 16" pan. Bake at 375° for 30 minutes or until done. While cake is baking, prepare icing.

Icing

Mix: 1 stick margarine
       3 Tbsp. cocoa
       6 Tbsp. milk.
Bring to boil and add:
       1 box confectioners' sugar
       1 tsp. vanilla
       ½ c. coarsely chopped walnuts
Spread over cake while hot. Serves 12 or more.

Brownie (easier than) Pie

No crust!

Beat to soft peaks: 3 egg whites

While continuing to beat, gradually add ¾ c. sugar and a dash of salt. Beat until stiff.

Fold in:
       ¾ c. chocolate wafer crumbs
       ½ c. broken walnuts
       ½ tsp. vanilla

Bake in 9" buttered pie tin at 325° for 30 – 35 minutes. Cool. Chill 3 hours to overnight. 2 – 3 hours before serving top with ½ pint heavy cream, whipped and sweetened. Chill and serve.

Carrot Cake

This is a good one!

Mix: 2 c. sugar

1½ c. cooking oil

4 eggs

Sift together and add:

2 c. flour

2 tsp. baking soda

1 tsp. salt

2 tsp. cinnamon

Mix well and add:

3 c. grated carrots

1 c. coconut

1 c. nuts

Pour into greased 9" x 13" pan and bake at 350° for 45 minutes or until done. Cool and frost.

Cream Cheese Frosting

Soften to room temperature:

1 8 oz. pkg. cream cheese

½ stick butter

Mix with:

2 tsp. vanilla

1 lb. confectioners sugar

Mix well and frost cooled cake.

Chilled Blueberry/Banana Pie

An unusual treat

1 baked 9" graham cracker crust (purchased or made from recipe following)

Line pie crust with slices from 2 bananas. Sprinkle with lemon juice to prevent darkening.

Soften 4 oz. cream cheese and whip with 2 Tbsp. sifted confectioners sugar and a touch of milk if needed to make it easy to spread. Fold in 4 oz. whipped topping and 1 tsp. vanilla and the grated peel of a lemon. Beat until well blended. Pour on bananas and chill.

Topping

Mix in saucepan:

1 c. blueberries

½ c. water

1 c. sugar

3 Tbsp. cornstarch

½ tsp. cinnamon

⅛ tsp. salt

Cook until thick. Remove from heat and add 1 c. blueberries

that have been sprinkled with 1 Tbsp. lemon juice. Add 1 Tbsp. butter. Cool and chill before adding a generous amount to each piece of pie.

Graham Cracker Crust

Quick and easy

Mix: 1½ c. graham cracker crumbs (about 10 crackers)

4 Tbsp. melted margarine

3 Tbsp. sugar

Press into pie pan. Bake at 350° for 10 min. Cool and add filling.

Lona's Lemon Angel Dessert

Beautiful as well as delicious

Dissolve: 1 pkg. plain gelatin in

4 Tbsp. cold water

Add: 1 c. boiling water

1 c. fresh orange juice

juice of 1 lemon and a touch of grated rind

¼ tsp. salt

⅔ c. sugar

Let set partially until it mounds. Fold in ½ pint heavy cream, whipped. Line medium sized mixing bowl with wax paper or plastic wrap. Tear pieces of angel-food cake, homemade or purchased, into 1 – 1½" pieces.

Put layer of cake in lined bowl. Spoon on some gelatin. Press down slightly, repeat until all is used. Let set overnight in refrigerator. Turn out, remove paper, and spread with ½ pint heavy cream, whipped and sweetened as desired.

Decorate with coconut and oranges, mint leaves, or any fruit and edible flowers such as Johnny Jump Ups.

Luscious Dessert Cake

So good it is hard to leave alone

Buy a yellow or lemon cake mix and prepare according to directions, or any old two-egg cake recipe will do as the topping is so good.

Heat oven to 350°. Instead of baking in regular cake pans, spread in a greased jelly roll pan, at least 11" x 15". Bake until done and browned on top (20 – 30 minutes or so).

When cool, top with cream cheese mixture, fruit, and whipped cream.

Cream cheese mixture

Whip an 8 oz. pkg. cream cheese, — may use light, or no-fat

Add: 3 ½ c. milk

2 small or 1 large pkg. instant pudding (vanilla or

Recipes

French vanilla)

    1 tsp. vanilla (or lemon extract)

Beat until smooth with electric mixer. Fold in 1 c. cream, whipped or 2 c. whipped topping. Top with any fruit — about 1 quart blueberries, 5 or 6 peaches, a couple of cans of drained pineapple, 4 or 5 bananas, or 1 qt. fresh strawberries or raspberries or any combination. Top with 1 c. heavy cream, whipped and sweetened. Chill before serving.

May's Strawberry Meringue Shortcake

What a sweet and fruity treat

Sift together:

    2 c. flour

    ¾ c. sugar

    2½ tsp. baking powder

    1 tsp. salt

Add: ⅓ c. shortening

    ½ c. milk

    1 tsp. vanilla

Beat 2 minutes. Add another ¼ c. milk and 2 egg yolks. Beat another minute and pour into a greased 9" x 13" pan.

Meringue for top:

Beat 2 egg whites until soft peaks form. Gradually add ½ c. sugar and ¼ tsp. cream of tartar, beating until stiff peaks form.

Bake at 300° for 40 – 50 minutes until toothpick comes out clean. Turn off oven and leave in until cool. Immediately before serving, top with sliced strawberries (fresh or frozen), and slightly sweetened whipped cream. Serves 12.

Meringue for pies

Makes enough for two

Have at room temperature in very large bowl:

    4 extra large egg whites

Add: ¼ tsp. cream of tartar

    ¼ tsp. salt

Beat until entire mixture is frothy.

Add: ½ tsp. vanilla

    ½ cup sugar, a little at a time, beating well after each addition.

Do not underbeat. Sugar must be dissolved. (The mixture will not be gritty between fingers when sugar is dissolved). Continue to beat until stiff pointed peaks form.

Place spoonfuls of meringue around edge of pies and spread so it touches the outside crust. Pile remainder of meringue in center of pies and spread to cover. Make peaks with a small spoon for an attractive look.

Bake at 350° until meringue peaks are golden brown. Cool gradually, away from drafts.

My Mom's Lemon Pie

Tart and delicious

Boil: 4 cups water

Mix: 2 c. sugar

    8 Tbsp. cornstarch

Add to boiling water. Stirring constantly, cook until clear and thick and add 2 tsp. butter. Cool slightly.

Add a small amount to 4 beaten extra large egg yolks. Then pour egg yolks into the rest of the pudding. Cook until done. It should come to a boil to be sure the eggs are done. Add the juice of 3 large lemons (at least 7 Tbsp. juice).

Pour into two 9" baked pie shells. Follow the recipe on page 122 or buy ready made. Top with meringue. (For a pineapple pie, decrease water to 3¼ c. and add 1 can (15 oz.) pineapple with the egg yolks.)

My Mom's Pumpkin Pie

Nice and spicy

In large saucepan, scald 2 cups milk. It is scalded when you blow gently on the surface and you see that a skin has started to form.

Add: 3 eggs, slightly beaten

    ½ c. brown sugar

    ½ c. white sugar

    ½ tsp. salt

    6 tsp. pumpkin pie spice

    1 large can (quart) pumpkin (or cook fresh and put it through a sieve)

Mix well and pour into 2 unbaked 9" pie crusts. A recipe for pie crusts can be found on page 122 or you can buy them ready made. Bake at 400° until crust starts to brown. Reduce heat to 350° and cook until knife inserted in center comes out clean. Serve as is or with whipped cream and a sprinkling of nuts that have been sprinkled with cinnamon, or with your favorite topping.

Quick Baked Pie Shell

When you're in a hurry

Pre-heat oven to 450°.

Mix :   1 c. prepackaged biscuit mix

    ¼ c. butter or margarine, softened

Add: 2 Tbsp. boiling water.

Stir vigorously until soft dough forms. Press dough firmly with floured hands into pie plate, 9" x 1½" bringing dough onto rim of plate, flute edges. Prick bottom of crust and bake 8 – 10 minutes. Cool.

Rhubarb Berry Cobbler

Think Spring

Combine in buttered 9" x 13" pan:

    4 c. diced rhubarb

    1 -16 oz. pkg. frozen strawberries

    ¾ c. sugar

Cream together in bowl:

    ½ c. butter

    1 c. sugar

Beat in 1 lightly beaten egg.

Sift: 2 c. flour

        3 tsp. baking powder

        ½ tsp. salt

Add flour mixture to sugar mixture alternately with 1 cup milk and 1 tsp. vanilla. Beat and spoon evenly over fruit. Bake at 350° for 40 – 50 minutes or until toothpick inserted in center of the topping comes out clean. Serve warm with ice cream or whipped cream, if desired. Serves 12.

Snacks, Cookies & Goodies

Annette's Moist Choco Cake

Everyone will love it

Cream: 2 c. sugar

         ½ c. margarine

Add: 2 eggs, well beaten

Sift: ⅔ c. cocoa

      2 c. flour

      3 tsp. baking soda

      1 tsp. baking powder

      1 tsp. salt

Add flour mixture to sugar mixture, alternating with 2 c. hot water. Add 2 tsp. vanilla. Batter will be very thin. Don't worry!

Bake at 350° in two greased and floured 8" round pans or one 9" x 13" pan for approximately 35 minutes for rounds and 45 minutes or so for large pan. Frost with your favorite frosting or serve with whipped cream.

Babs' Gingersnap Cookies

Deliciously spicy

Cream: ¾ c. shortening

        1 c. sugar

Add   ¼ c. molasses

        1 egg

Sift and add:

      2 c. flour

      2 tsp. soda

      1 tsp. cloves

      1 tsp. cinnamon

      1 tsp. ginger

      ¼ tsp. salt

Roll in small balls and bake at 325° for approximately 10 minutes. Makes 4 dozen.

Candy Popcorn

Once you start munching, you can't stop

Melt: 1 cup butter

Stir in: 2 c. brown sugar

        ½ c. corn syrup

        1 tsp. salt

Bring to boil, stirring constantly. Boil without stirring, 5 minutes. Remove from heat.

Stir in: ½ tsp. baking soda

        2 tsp. vanilla

Carefully stir into 6 qts. popped corn and 1 c. honey roasted peanuts (optional). Turn into large roasting pan or two baking pans. Bake at 250° for 45 minutes, stirring every 15 minutes. Cool completely and break apart.

Chocolate Mint Chip Cookies

Cool, refreshing mint makes these a real treat

Cream: 1¼ c. margarine

        2 c. sugar

Add: 2 eggs

        2 tsp. vanilla

Sift together and add:

      2 c. flour

      ¾ c. baking cocoa

      1 tsp. baking soda

      ½ tsp salt

Mix in 1 large package mint chocolate chips.

Chill at least an hour in refrigerator. Bake at 350° for 8 minutes. Do not overbake.

Double Chocolate Brownies

Decadent and delicious

Melt: ¾ c. margarine

Stir in: ¾ c. baking cocoa and cool.

Recipes

Beat until light:

      4 eggs

      ¼ tsp. salt

Beat in 2 c. sugar gradually until creamy.

Add: melted mixture

      1 tsp. vanilla

      1 c. all-purpose flour

Beat until smooth.

Fold in 1 c. nuts and 1 c. chocolate chips. Pour into greased 9" x 13" pan. Bake at 325° for 30 minutes.

Elsie's Oatmeal Crisps

Old fashioned crispy oat cookies

Cream:

      2 c. shortening

      2 c. brown sugar

      2 c. white sugar

      2 tsp. vanilla

Add: 4 eggs one at a time

Sift and add:

      3 c. flour

      2 tsp. salt

      2 tsp. soda

      6 c. rolled oats (not quick oats)

Drop on ungreased baking sheet. Bake at 350° for 8 –12 minutes.

Lemon Blueberry Zucchini Snack Bread

Zucchini can be grated and frozen for wintertime baking

Mix together:

      3 c. all-purpose flour

      1½ c. sugar

      4½ tsp. baking powder

      1 tsp. salt

Mix in separate bowl:

      4 eggs

      ⅔ c. vegetable oil

      2 c. grated zucchini

      2 tsp. grated lemon peel

      1 tsp. lemon extract

Make a well in the dry ingredients. Pour liquid into well and stir until moistened. Fold in: 1 c. fresh blueberries (or well-drained frozen berries).

Pour batter into two bread pans (approximately 8"x 4"). Bake at 350° 45 – 60 minutes. Cool slightly on wire racks and remove from pan.

Sand Cookies

Easy rolled cookies

Cream: 1 c. margarine

      1½ c. sugar

Add: 2 eggs

      ½ tsp. baking soda dissolved in 1 Tbsp. water

      2 tsp. vanilla

Stir in: 4 c. flour

Roll out dough about ⅛" thick and cut out. Sprinkle with cinnamon sugar. Baked on greased cookie sheet at 375° for 8 minutes.

Sue's Chocolate Chip Oatmeal Cookies

Easy to double for a crowd

Cream: 1 c. margarine

      ¾ c. brown sugar

      ¾ c. sugar

Mix together and add to above:

      2 c. flour

      2 tsp. baking soda

      1 tsp. salt

Add and mix until moist:

      2 eggs

      2 tsp. vanilla

Stir in: 3 c. quick oats

      2 c. (12 oz.) chocolate chips

Drop by teaspoonful onto an ungreased cookie sheet, and bake at 350° for 8 – 10 minutes. Or, shape into rolls, wrap in plastic wrap, and freeze. When company drops in, just slice and bake for 15 minutes for fresh, hot cookies on the spot.

AQS Books on Quilts

This is only a partial listing of the books on quilts that are available from the American Quilter's Society. AQS books are known the world over for their timely topics, clear writing, beautiful color photographs, and accurate illustrations and patterns. The following books are available from your local bookseller, quilt shop, or public library. If you are unable to locate certain titles in your area, you may order by mail from the AMERICAN QUILTER'S SOCIETY, P.O. Box 3290, Paducah, KY 42002-3290. Add $2.00 for postage for the first book ordered and 40¢ for each additional book. Include item number, title, and price when ordering. Allow 14 to 21 days for delivery. Customers with Visa, MasterCard, or Discover may phone in orders from 7:00–5:00 CST, Monday–Friday, Toll Free 1-800-626-5420.

4595	**Above & Beyond Basics,** Karen Kay Buckley	$18.95
2282	**Adapting Architectural Details for Quilts,** Carol Wagner	$12.95
4813	**Addresses & Birthdays,** compiled by Klaudeen Hansen **(HB)**	$14.95
4543	**American Quilt Blocks: 50 Patterns for 50 States,** Beth Summers	$16.95
4696	**Amish Kinder Komforts,** Bettina Havig	$14.95
4829	**Anita Shackelford: Surface Textures,** Anita Shackelford **(HB)**	$24.95
4899	**Appliqué Paper Greetings,** Elly Sienkiewicz **(HB)**	$24.95
3790	**Appliqué Patterns from Native American Beadwork Designs,** Dr. Joyce Mori	$14.95
2099	**Ask Helen: More About Quilting Designs,** Helen Squire	$14.95
2207	**Award-Winning Quilts: 1985-1987**	$24.95
2354	**Award-Winning Quilts: 1988-1989**	$24.95
3425	**Award-Winning Quilts: 1990-1991**	$24.95
3791	**Award-Winning Quilts: 1992-1993**	$24.95
4593	**Blossoms by the Sea: Making Ribbon Flowers for Quilts,** Faye Labanaris	$24.95
4697	**Caryl Bryer Fallert: A Spectrum of Quilts, 1983-1995,** Caryl Bryer Fallert	$24.95
4626	**Celtic Geometric Quilts,** Camille Remme	$16.95
3926	**Celtic Style Floral Appliqué,** Scarlett Rose	$14.95
2208	**Classic Basket Quilts,** Elizabeth Porter & Marianne Fons	$16.95
2355	**Creative Machine Art,** Sharee Dawn Roberts	$24.95
4818	**Dear Helen, Can You Tell Me?** Helen Squire	$15.95
3399	**Dye Painting!** Ann Johnston	$19.95
4814	**Encyclopedia of Designs for Quilting,** Phyllis D. Miller **(HB)**	$34.95
3468	**Encyclopedia of Pieced Quilt Patterns,** compiled by Barbara Brackman	$34.95
3846	**Fabric Postcards,** Judi Warren	$22.95
4594	**Firm Foundations,** Jane Hall & Dixie Haywood	$18.95
4900	**Four Blocks Continued…,** Linda Giesler Carlson	$16.95
2381	**From Basics to Binding,** Karen Kay Buckley	$16.95
4526	**Gatherings: America's Quilt Heritage,** Kathlyn F. Sullivan	$34.95
2097	**Heirloom Miniatures,** Tina M. Gravatt	$9.95
4628	**Helen's Guide to quilting in the 21st century,** Helen Squire	$16.95
1906	**Irish Chain Quilts: A Workbook of Irish Chains,** Joyce B. Peaden	$14.95
3784	**Jacobean Appliqué: Book I, "Exotica,"** Campbell & Ayars	$18.95
4544	**Jacobean Appliqué: Book II, "Romantica,"** Campbell & Ayars	$18.95
3904	**The Judge's Task,** Patricia J. Morris	$19.95
4751	**Liberated Quiltmaking,** Gwen Marston **(HB)**	$24.95
4897	**Lois Smith's Machine Quiltmaking,** Lois Smith	$19.95
4523	**Log Cabin Quilts: New Quilts from an Old Favorite**	$14.95
4545	**Log Cabin with a Twist,** Barbara T. Kaempfer	$18.95
4815	*Love to Quilt:* **Bears, Bears, Bears,** Karen Kay Buckley	$14.95
4833	*Love to Quilt:* **Broderie Perse: The Elegant Quilt,** Barbara W. Barber	$14.95
4598	*Love to Quilt:* **Men's Vests,** Alexandra Capadalis Dupré	$14.95
4816	*Love to Quilt:* **Necktie Sampler Blocks,** Janet B. Elwin	$14.95
4753	*Love to Quilt:* **Penny Squares,** Willa Baranowski	$12.95
4911	**Mariner's Compass Quilts: New Quilts from an Old Favorite**	$16.95
4752	**Miniature Quilts: Connecting New & Old Worlds,** Tina M. Gravatt	$14.95
4514	**Mola Techniques for Today's Quilters,** Charlotte Patera	$18.95
3330	**More Projects and Patterns,** Judy Florence	$18.95
1981	**Nancy Crow: Quilts and Influences,** Nancy Crow	$29.95
3331	**Nancy Crow: Work in Transition,** Nancy Crow	$12.95
4828	**Nature, Design & Silk Ribbons,** Cathy Grafton	$18.95
3332	**New Jersey Quilts,** The Heritage Quilt Project of New Jersey	$29.95
3927	**New Patterns from Old Architecture,** Carol Wagner	$12.95
2153	**No Dragons on My Quilt,** Jean Ray Laury	$12.95
4627	**Ohio Star Quilts: New Quilts from an Old Favorite**	$16.95
3469	**Old Favorites in Miniature,** Tina Gravatt	$15.95
4831	**Optical Illusions for Quilters,** Karen Combs	$22.95
4515	**Paint and Patches: Painting on Fabrics with Pigment,** Vicki L. Johnson	$18.95
3333	**A Patchwork of Pieces,** complied by Benberry & Crabb	$14.95
4513	**Plaited Patchwork,** Shari Cole	$19.95
3928	**Precision Patchwork for Scrap Quilts,** Jeannette Tousley Muir	$12.95
4779	**Protecting Your Quilts: A Guide for Quilt Owners, Second Edition**	$6.95
4542	**A Quilted Christmas,** edited by Bonnie Browning	$18.95
2380	**Quilter's Registry,** Lynne Fritz	$9.95
3467	**Quilting Patterns from Native American Designs,** Dr. Joyce Mori	$12.95
3470	**Quilting with Style,** Gwen Marston & Joe Cunningham	$24.95
2284	**Quiltmaker's Guide: Basics & Beyond,** Carol Doak	$19.95
4918	**Quilts by Paul D. Pilgrim: Blending the Old & the New,** Gerald E. Roy	$16.95
2257	*Quilts:* **The Permanent Collection – MAQS**	$9.95
3793	*Quilts:* **The Permanent Collection – MAQS Volume II**	$9.95
3789	**Roots, Feathers & Blooms,** Linda Giesler Carlson	$16.95
4512	**Sampler Quilt Blocks from Native American Designs,** Dr. Joyce Mori	$14.95
3796	**Seasons of the Heart & Home: Quilts for a Winter's Day,** Jan Patek	$18.95
3761	**Seasons of the Heart & Home: Quilts for Summer Days,** Jan Patek	$18.95
2357	**Sensational Scrap Quilts,** Darra Duffy Williamson	$24.95
3375	**Show Me Helen…How to Use Quilting Designs,** Helen Squire	$15.95
4783	**Silk Ribbons by Machine,** Jeanie Sexton	$15.95
3929	**The Stori Book of Embellishing,** Mary Stori	$16.95
3903	**Straight Stitch Machine Appliqué,** Letty Martin	$16.95
3792	**Striplate Piecing,** Debra Wagner	$24.95
3930	**Tessellations & Variations,** Barbara Ann Caron	$14.95
3788	**Three-Dimensional Appliqué and Embroidery Embellishment: Techniques for Today's Album Quilt,** Anita Shackelford	$24.95
4596	**Ties, Ties, Ties: Traditional Quilts from Neckties,** Janet B. Elwin	$19.95
3931	**Time-Span Quilts: New Quilts from Old Tops,** Becky Herdle	$16.95
2029	**A Treasury of Quilting Designs,** Linda Goodmon Emery	$14.95
3847	**Tricks with Chintz,** Nancy S. Breland	$14.95
2286	**Wonderful Wearables: A Celebration of Creative Clothing,** Virginia Avery	$24.95
4812	**Who's Who in American Quilting,** edited by Bonnie Browning **(HB)**	$49.95
4956	**Variegreat! New Dimensions in Traditional Quilts,** Linda Glantz	$19.95
4972	**20th Century Quilts,** Cuesta Benberry and Joyce Gross	$ 9.95

May T. Miller

May was brought up on a small remote dairy farm in Delaware County, New York, situated in the foothills of the Catskill Mountains. When she was ten, having no electricity, she started making her own clothing on a treadle sewing machine. After high school, May became a cosmetologist but had little time to practice her profession as she soon married a dairy farmer and spent the next 26 years helping operate their farm in Franklin, New York.

In the early eighties, May and her sister Betty opened an antiques shop on Main Street. In 1984 May took a beginner's quilting class and as they say — the rest is history. The antiques were soon replaced with quilting fabric, and May began teaching quilting classes with the help of Betty and a friend, Babs Butts.

After selling the dairy farm and moving to a farm a few miles away, the quilt shop was moved to a remodeled chicken house on the Millers' new property. Classes are held at the shop, and it is open by appointment. One of May's newest ventures is the introduction of Scrap Magic™, quilting pattern sheets.

Susan B. Burton

Sue Burton grew up with handmade quilts on every bed and has always loved beautiful quilts. Though still an amateur quilter, she always has a project or two in the works and readily admits enjoying the planning and piecing of a quilt far more than the quilting itself. She is an accomplished weaver and belongs to the Handweavers of Bucks County Guild.

As an editor and communications specialist, Sue enjoys simplifying the complex so that even beginners can turn out a product they will be proud to say they made. She has used her computer design skills to collaborate on a pattern kit produced by Everything Else.

Sue lives in New Tripoli, Pennsylvania, with her husband, daughter, cat, and Border Collie.